Jerilyn,

Happy New Year! Thanks for all your support & partnership this past year! Best, Dr. Greg

TRAPPED IN THE BIG EASY

A Hurricane, Leadership from the Heart,

and the Quest for a Life of Purpose

GREGORY A. KETCHUM PH.D.

TALENTPLANET PUBLISHING®
MUIR BEACH, CA.

Trapped in the Big Easy

A TalentPlanet Publishing® Book / December 2013

Copyright © 2013 by Gregory A. Ketchum Ph.D.

Printed in the United States of America. For permission requests, write to the publisher, addressed "Attention Permissions Coordinator," at the address below

TalentPlanet Publishing®
88 Seacape Dr.,
Muir Beach, CA. 94965
www.talentplanet.com

Library of Congress Control Number: 2013956095
ISBN: 9780991220007 (paperback)
ISBN: 9780991220014 (ePub)
ISBN: 0991220005

Book cover design by Andrea Design Group, S.F., CA.
Proofreaders: Debbie Hurt, Mike Ketchum, Larry Hoose, Katie Nittler
Editor: Marlene Mahoney

The names of most, but not all, of the people mentioned in this book have been changed.

DEDICATION

This book is lovingly dedicated to my family, especially to the love of my life, Debbie, and to my children. You all inspire me, fill me with pride, and bring joy to my life every single day.

Kaitlin's apartment windows all taped up and ready to meet Katrina.

CONTENTS

Acknowledgments

I have so many people to thank for helping make the dream of publishing this book a reality. Special thanks to Debbie Hurt for her unwavering support, inspiration, love, and belief in me. Larry Hoose and Gail Baxter Pollard deserve special notice for their encouragement and for being my very first readers when the book was just a blog. Thanks to my daughter, Kaitlin, who has been my wonderful traveling buddy on our many adventures in New Orleans. Jim Krasula is my guardian angel who rescued me from New Orleans. I can never thank him enough for his kindness when I needed it most. My brothers, Steve, Mike, and Brian have always been there for me even back to the days in our backyard in Steele. Marlene Mahoney has provided tons of encouragement along with her fantastic editing skills. Thanks, Marlene, for taking this trip with me as we worked on the book together. Michelle Maldonado has given me wonderful support, especially in getting the word out on the book. Andrea Griffin has done a magnificent job conveying the feeling of what the book is about by creating just the right cover design. Marge Josephson has been a key supporter of this book project and by sharing her love of New Orleans has provided another heart link to that glorious city. Many wonderful people of New Orleans and surrounding areas helped me during the my entire Katrina ordeal and I wouldn't have made it through without them. A special heartfelt thanks goes out to my lovely and dear New Orleans, one of the great cities of the world.

Finally, publication of this book would not have been possible without the generous support and love of our friends, colleagues, and family members who pledged to our *Kickstarter* campaign. Massive heartfelt thanks to Jason and Clarissa Smigell, Brandon Hurt, Ashley Crenshaw, Debbie Hurt, Mike and Patty Ketchum, Blake and Monica Ketchum, Larry and Debra Hoose, Kecia Mortenson and Kevin Pound, Keith and Kathy Mar, Jared Worthen, David Steele and Heidi Mixson, Babak Hemati and Noushin Oshidari, Claudia and Michael Fergang, Al and Jill Malinchak, Bonnie Jean Shelton, Diane Dearmore, Neal and Joanna Rogers, Joy Fillman, Diane Pomerantz, Paula Cardaleen, Allison Michels, Steve Polito and Sara Carter, Sandra Hrabovsky Bevill, Arizona Lugon, Ahmad Omais, Gay Colyer, Linda Schenk, Julie and Brent Smith, Marie Minder, Richard Sheppard, Pat Burns, Mark McLean, Bobby Childs, Scott McPhail, Paul and Anne Jeschke, Sydnie Kohara, Tonya Tokar, Jenise Bobo, John Warren, Brock Whisenhunt Sr., Charla Parker, Mary Anne Caldwell, Cris Ray, Marge Josephson, Sale Schille, Mark Munley, Jenny Callicott, Pam Marrs, Paul De Young, and Jorge Rey-Prada.

INTRODUCTION

Long after the images of suffering, confusion, and death from Hurricane Katrina recede from public memory this one fact will remain; the story of Katrina is one of the massive failure of leadership on all levels of government: local, state and federal. Had strong leadership been on the ground in New Orleans on the afternoon of the storm, much of the looting, suffering, and death could have been prevented.

How would I know? I was there in the French quarter from four days before to four days after Katrina struck. After the winds and rain had stopped I saw firsthand the looting of the Walgreens next to my hotel on Rue Royal. I watched as people on the street cheered one looter after another as they emerged from the store with double armfuls of merchandise. I experienced the unbearable heat, the absence of electricity and running water, the shortages of food and drinking water, the rumors, the uncertainty of what was going to happen next, and of when or how we'd be able to escape. I heard more than one person exclaim in a fit of frustration, "This is the United States of America. This isn't supposed to be happening here!"

I watched as civil order broke down. The first time I saw any National Guard troops was four days after Katrina struck as I was leaving the city. They were in a defensive posture setting up a command post at the Embassy Suites Hotel. The soldiers standing guard in full battle gear, weapons at the ready, had stone cold faces, the "don't-approach-me-and-don't-make-any-rapid-moves-or-I'll-blow-you-away" look. I never saw any representatives of the Red Cross or Salvation Army or any other aid organization the entire time I was there. And how about the New Orleans police? Since getting out I've heard many stories of heroic acts by the police, but I didn't witness any of those myself. I'm still trying to figure out where most of the police were and what they were doing. I would see them bunched up guarding the media trucks or racing by in their squad cars, but never stopping to offer aid.

This book is about what it was like to be trapped in a major American city with a Category 4 or 5 hurricane bearing down on you. It's also a story about leadership, it's failures, and five primary leadership lessons I learned about developing the ability to lead from your intuition and heart. Finally, *Trapped in the Big Easy* is the story of being catapulted onto the search for a life of purpose along with the challenges to keeping faith on that journey.

I hope you enjoy the trip and discover lessons that you can apply to your own life quest.

ONE

How I Got to New Orleans

S ometimes the chance to face yourself and discover your natural leadership instincts forces itself on you. That's what happened to me. My "leadership chance" happened when I found myself stuck in a luxury French Quarter hotel unable to leave New Orleans, just waiting to get clobbered by Hurricane Katrina.

My daughter, Kaitlin, was about to start her sophomore year at Loyola University in New Orleans and was home for the summer in the San Francisco Bay Area. She wanted to take her car to school so we planned a "father-daughter" road trip across country. On the morning of Saturday, August 21, 2005, we set out for New Orleans in her red 2000 VW Beetle that we affectionately called "Little Red."

We arrived in New Orleans on Thursday evening, August 25th and made our way to her little apartment near Loyola in the Garden District. It was hot as hell and since her room had been shut off all summer it was stifling. We unloaded the car and turned on the window air conditioner, but it was going to take several hours to cool the room. I had planned to stay, but it was so hot that I decided to book a room at the Hotel Monteleone, a 129 year old family owned French Quarter hotel, where I'd stayed when I brought Kaitlin down to start

1

her Freshman year. Kaitlin, anxious to get started on setting up her room, decided to stay in the apartment.

I was due to fly back to San Francisco on Sunday, August 28th on Southwest leaving at 5:20 pm so we had a couple of days to get Kaitlin settled into her apartment. Although we didn't realize it at the time, Hurricane Katrina was headed for New Orleans, expected to hit on the following Monday.

On Friday, August 26th, our first full day in New Orleans, we joined all the other college students and their parents at Target, stocking up on supplies and furniture. Without knowing it, we found ourselves part of a yearly ritual, something much bigger than our own plans, of parents setting up college base camps for their kids. It took awhile to get used to the summer heat and humidity. What made it bearable were the little breaks in the air-conditioned car and air-conditioned store. Otherwise, the breath was sucked right out of us.

Several hundred dollars later we got back to Kaitlin's apartment where we both got busy setting up her room. Kaitlin unpacked and cleaned while I put together her new fan, vacuum cleaner, bookcase and table. We had the TV on in the background, and occasionally we'd hear something about some hurricane down in Florida. We really paid it no mind and continued to work until we were exhausted, sweaty, and starving.

After grabbing a snack, I left Kaitlin and drove down St. Charles Avenue to the French Quarter and parked in the hotel garage. I loved walking into the lobby of the Monteleone with her stately elegance, old world charm, and gorgeous crystal chandeliers. The beauty of the place along with the friendliness of the staff evoked such feelings of comfort, order, and welcome that I sat down on one of the beautiful sofas just to enjoy the atmosphere and soak in the elegance. It was a welcome treat after spending the day working in the heat to get Kaitlin's room ready.

I finally made my way up to my room and settled down for the night determined to sleep-in the next morning, Saturday, to catch up from the wear and tear of the drive cross country. The air conditioning felt oh so good as did the nice cleanly starched white sheets. I reveled in the feeling of being enveloped in cool luxury as I drifted off to sleep.

TWO

Getting the News to Evacuate

The Next Morning, Saturday, August 27, 2005. Two Days
Before Katrina

I was awakened by a call from an excited Kaitlin telling me that
Hurricane Katrina was now headed for New Orleans, that a mandatory evacuation was in effect, and that we had to leave right away.
What? Wasn't the hurricane over by Florida? Was she sure that we had
to really leave? Shouldn't we stay and see how things developed? Maybe
it wouldn't really hit New Orleans. Besides that, the storm wasn't due
until Monday morning. I told her I'd call her in a few minutes after
I checked the television. She repeated that we really didn't have any
time to waste and that she needed to pick me up now. I assured her
that I'd call right back.

I flipped on the TV to all-Hurricane-all-the-time-coverage. The
President of Jefferson Parish, next door to Orleans Parish, was urging everyone to leave, having already declared a mandatory evacuation. On another channel, New Orleans Mayor Ray Nagin sat at the
anchor desk with two news correspondents for a local station, saying
that there was no mandatory evacuation in effect for Orleans Parish.
People could leave if they wanted, but he was taking a "wait and see"

approach. More channel flipping revealed breathless correspondents in front of already jammed freeways reporting that, "this could be the one that we've always feared," and "experts are calling this a Category 5 hurricane that could wreak unimaginable damage on the Crescent City." More channel flipping and I was watching discussions of just when "contra-flow" measures would go into effect. That's when all of the freeways headed into New Orleans are reversed to carry traffic headed out only. By mid-day Saturday all freeway lanes now led out of the city and were jammed solid. People who'd run out of gas had to just push their cars over to the side of the freeway and hope for the best.

Kaitlin called back and I told her to pick me up. I got my things together, checked out and met Kaitlin in the garage of the Monteleone. We drove Little Red down St. Charles Avenue out towards her apartment on Henry Clay Street. Along the way, we made a couple of stops: one at a Shell station to fill up and the other at a Rite Aid to pick up whatever emergency items were left on the shelves. There was already a line of cars at the gas station adding to a growing sense of tension and competition for supplies. The Rite Aid was crowded with people and everyone seemed to be carrying several gallons of water to the check out stand. Flashlights, batteries and snack food were the other popular items. We grabbed a couple of six packs of water, several quarts of motor oil, some snacks and most importantly a couple of bottles of red wine. I told Kaitlin that, "The storm might be driving us out of New Orleans, but we aren't going without wine."

We got to Kaitlin's apartment, and she got her things together to leave town. Both Kaitlin and her roommate, Coco, displayed a sense of urgency to get on the road *now* that I didn't quite understand. However, they had both been forced to evacuate a year prior when Hurricane Ivan threatened New Orleans by driving north to Baton Rouge, a drive that normally takes an hour and a half, but on that day took nearly nine. They weren't eager to go through that again.

On the other hand, I was still undecided about leaving and several factors weighed on my mind. First, I had just spent six days in the car and wasn't eager to get back in for the congested drive to Houston, one which normally takes about six hours, but given the circumstances, God only knew how long it would take. Second, Kaitlin had three of her college girlfriends with her, and I felt like the tag-along Dad. They had another car in addition to Little Red, but still I hesitated. If you have kids in college you know what I'm talking about as far as not wanting to "intrude." It was maybe a silly consideration given the circumstances, but there it was running around inside my head nonetheless. Third, I had a flight set on Southwest the next afternoon, the day before the storm was due, and confirmed–and was assured—that my flight was still scheduled. Finally, and this one is hard to admit, there was a little piece of me that wanted to experience a hurricane. I wouldn't have admitted that to my wife, Kathy, but sure enough, there it was, the thrill seeker wanting to know just what that would be like. However, my little adventurer didn't even think about what would happen once the storm passed. I figured I'd give the Feds and the Red Cross the day off for the storm and would see them on Tuesday, the day after.

THREE

BATTENING DOWN KAITLIN'S APARTMENT

Saturday, August 27, 2005. Two Days Before Katrina.

Standing in Kaitlin's sweltering apartment, undecided about staying or going, we still had to batten everything down. Her room was a mess of bags, books, clothes, and half-put together pieces of furniture. The bookcase that I'd been putting together had to be laid flat on the floor so as to not get blown down if a window shattered. The windows, the old wooden casement style that had seen better days, swung outward. The latches were broken and the only way to secure them was to tie string or wire around the latches to hold them together. I knew this wouldn't work, but with no time to run to the hardware store I had to make do with what the girls had around the apartment. I had Kaitlin bring me their "tool box" that one of the other "dads" had put together, and I found some screws and other bits of metal that I crafted into anchors for the windows. I secured Kaitlin's as best I could and then went to the front bedroom, Cat's room, to try to secure her windows, which were in much worse shape than Kaitlin's. Her room had been shut off from the rest of the house and was so hot that bead after bead of sweat dripped down and hung off the end of my nose before dropping onto the floor.

Once we'd done what we could to secure the apartment, Kaitlin and her friends got ready to drive to Houston. She was taking Little Red and her roommate, Coco, was taking her car. Seeing that she was okay, I told her that I was going to stay, check back into the Monteleone and catch my Southwest flight the next day. She didn't really protest which signaled to me that she was fine with it.

I had to get back to the French Quarter and the girls were leaving New Orleans in the opposite direction. I didn't want to hold them up so I had Kaitlin drop me off on St. Charles Avenue by the streetcar line. I got out of the car, kissed Kaitlin goodbye and told them to be careful. I watched them drive away as I stood on the corner of St. Charles and Henry Clay with my briefcase over my shoulder, holding my bag in one hand and a couple of shirts on hangers in dry cleaning bags in other. There was no turning back now and no other way out of New Orleans except for my flight the next day. I had chosen.

I walked to the nearest streetcar stop and waited in the heat for about ten minutes for the next trolley. I moved through the full car and found a seat in back. The sun was out and it was hard to comprehend that a Category 5 storm was headed our way. Everything seemed so normal that it was all a bit surreal. Not a single person on that car looked worried, and I didn't overhear anyone talking about the approaching storm.

The ride down to the Quarter took about fifteen minutes and the walk to the Monteleone was only a couple of blocks from there. I got to the hotel, checked back in and put my things in the room before going out to explore the Quarter. They had given me a room on the 4th floor that faced the Rue Royal and the building across the street. There are always lots of street musicians playing in the Quarter and sure enough there was one on the corner right then, playing an electric guitar that was loud and frightful. This wasn't going to work I told myself, so I called and asked the front desk if they had another room away from the street noise. They did have one and told me to come for a new room card.

I switched room key cards and then caught the elevator up to my new room, #1572, on the top floor of the hotel. I entered and found that it was quiet and had a nice view of the city. "This is much better," I thought.

FOUR

THE CALM BEFORE THE STORM

Saturday, August 27, 2005. Two Days Before Katrina.

It was now mid-afternoon on Saturday and the storm was predicted to hit around 6:30 a.m. on Monday morning. I called Southwest to check on my flight, and the reservation agent told me that they expected to be flying on Sunday, but that I should call back in the morning to confirm. As far as I was concerned, I had a day to check out New Orleans and the Quarter and to see what a city looked like that was about to be walloped by a Category 5 hurricane. You know, that would make a great story, me in New Orleans narrowly escaping Hurricane Katrina, likely on one of the last flights out of the city. I started taking notes in my head.

Once I had settled into my room, I decided to see what was happening around the Quarter. On my way out of the hotel, I stopped in the lobby and got $200 out of the ATM figuring that was more than enough to hold me until my flight. I hit the street and it was a gorgeous, although very hot, sunny day, and life in the Quarter was going on like nothing in the world could be wrong. The bars were open, crowds were milling about with drinks in hand, and the music was blaring. Hey, it's New Orleans!

Just a few steps out of the hotel onto Rue Royal I reached up to adjust my sunglasses and the right ear piece broke off. Well, that wouldn't do in this blazing sun, so I went to Walgreens next door to pick up a new pair. The sunglass rack was just inside the door and after several spins of the rack I found a pair for $12.99. Suitably armed, I headed back out into the sun.

I walked the block to Bourbon Street, and the tourists and locals had the booze flowing. Some stores were boarding up windows or at least moving items out of the window showcases. Other than that, it was hard to see any real concern that Katrina was on its way. I did notice, however, fewer people in the streets.

Next I walked down to Jackson Square and Cafe du Monde where I sat and enjoyed coffee and beignets. Sitting there, I was again struck by how normal everything seemed. Even though I'd watched the frantic news reports about this being a "Category 5" storm and "the one we've always feared," I was easily lulled into a false sense of normalcy. I guess that's part of the mind-set that people can get into prior to a natural disaster striking. You know, looking around you see other people who don't seem to be panicked and so you feel silly for "overreacting" or "taking it too seriously," so you end up feeling less worried about it than you should. At least I did.

FIVE

WAITING FOR KATRINA

Sunday, August 28, 2005. One Day Before Katrina.

I woke up on Sunday morning and flipped on the television to catch the latest on the approaching storm. It was, of course, "all Katrina all the time" on the local stations. Finally, I caught Mayor Nagin announcing that a mandatory evacuation for Orleans Parish was now in effect. This seemed to me to be too late. I mean, by not making a mandatory announcement and showing some leadership the day before as the head of Jefferson Parish had, the Mayor implied that the storm might not be that bad. The day before when I had seen Mayor Nagin discussing the storm. I was thinking, "Who is this guy and why is he on TV?" When the anchor said at the end of the interview that they'd been speaking with the mayor, I was flabbergasted. If this is the guy who's in charge, then we're screwed.

I called Southwest around 10:30 a.m. to check on my flight and everything looked good, so I decided to take one last tour around the Quarter before heading to the airport. I walked down Rue Royal, the street that my hotel was on (the street cars once ran down it within hearing distance of the apartment of a young writer named Tennessee Williams) and stopped at Cafe Beignet for breakfast. It was hot already so I picked what seemed to be the coolest table. You know, that's what you do when you're someplace like New Orleans in August, you try to find the coolest seat in the house.

I had bought the Sunday edition of *The Times-Picayune* and settled in to read about the storm. The big bold letters on the front page read, "Katrina Takes Aim" with sub-headings that read, "An Extreme Storm: Monday landfall likely as strong Category 4," "Get on the Road: Officials strongly urging residents to leave area," "Wall of Water: Levees could be topped in the entire metro area." Finally, as if the message wasn't getting through, the last headline down the page read, "Katrina bulks up to become a perfect storm." Digging into the lead article just before my beignets, I read the following: "Katrina was expected to approach the area as a Category 4 storm, with winds of 145 mph, and it could build to a top-of-the-chart Category 5 storm, with winds of 155 mph or higher..." Man, I thought, was I glad that I was getting out of town just in the nick of time.

I finished breakfast and walked around the Quarter, and I could tell that something was up. There were fewer people and many stores were already closed or had never opened like the Walgreens. Yet, there was no sense of panic, but rather just a "we've been through this before" feeling. However, when I found that both McDonalds and Krystal Burger were closed, I knew it was serious. The Quarter was beginning to close up and seal itself off.

When I got back to the hotel, the first thing I did was go to the ATM and get another $200 cash, just in case. I went to my room and by now it was around 1:30 pm. I wasn't sure if I could find a cab to get to the airport, so I thought I'd better leave a bit early. However, I wasn't going to the airport until I was sure my flight was actually going to leave, so I called Southwest one more time. The reservation agent told me that the last flight out of the city was leaving around 2:15 pm and that everything after that was cancelled. No one else was flying out of New Orleans after that. "What do you mean that all flights are cancelled?" I stammered, "The storm isn't due until Monday morning. We've got plenty of time."

"Yes sir" she acknowledged, "but all flight operations will cease as of that last flight today. We need time to get our people out." I asked her when they'd be resuming normal operations and she guessed Tuesday after the storm. Being the optimist, I booked a seat on the same flight for Tuesday, August 30th, the very next day after the storm was due to hit.

So that was it. My life suddenly changed from "waiting for my flight out" to "waiting for Katrina" and let me tell you waiting for a Category 5 storm is pretty damned anxiety provoking. That little part of me that wanted to see what it was like to go through a major hurricane had gotten its wish. The rest of me, however, was not happy about that, so I immediately started calling rental car agencies. No sir, there are no cars available. People had even been renting U-Haul trucks to drive out of town and those are all gone too.

Now what was I going to do? I got on the phone to let my wife know that I wouldn't be coming home and she was not happy to hear that. There was nothing I could do except get ready for the storm. Would it blow out my windows or blow off the roof? I had no idea, but just the thoughts scared me.

Six

Getting Ready Sunday Afternoon

August 28, 2005. The Last Day Before Katrina.

I t's around 3 p.m. Now that I knew I wasn't going anywhere, I switched into "get ready" mode and decided to go and find food and water to stock in my room. I caught the elevator and when I came out into the lobby, I noticed that it was filling up fast with people, many of them African-American, who either had suitcases or bundles of belongings piled at their feet. There were so many people that all of the available seats were filled while others stood around and talked in small groups. Just about everyone was wearing a coat and holding bags of what looked like personal belongings in their hands. It was becoming difficult to walk through the lobby without having to stop every few feet to excuse myself just to get through. Something about this whole scene didn't fit as they didn't look like the usual guests I'd see at the Monteleone. It evoked an odd almost claustrophobic feeling in me.

I stopped and asked the concierge what was going on, and she told me that since the hotel had been there for 129 years and had been through many hurricanes, it was used as a refuge for indigents who had no way to get out of town. She also said that some members of the staff were moving their families into the hotel as well.

This influx of people from many of the poor neighborhoods into a Four Star luxury hotel as a Category 5 hurricane bore down on us on a gorgeous sunny day only added to the "surreal" nature of the whole experience. As I was standing in that lobby, those surreal elements started to pile up and push my sense of "normalcy" out the window. At the same time, excitement, fear, and a feeling of disequilibrium were being sucked into that space in my head that "normalcy" usually occupied. This was only the beginning of many strange experiences that Katrina brought with her to New Orleans.

I came out of the hotel onto Rue Royal to look for supplies. By now most stores were boarded up or were in the process of putting up the plywood. I walked the half block to the next intersection and there was a guy sitting on a little wooden box right in the middle of Rue Royal, playing an electric guitar through a small old amplifier. Sheez, I thought, this guy sure doesn't look worried about the storm, and another surreal moment added to the fast growing pile.

I walked on and noticed a man coming my direction, carrying a couple of bulging plastic shopping bags in each hand. He looked like he had just bought the stuff, so I stopped and asked him where he got it. He told me that there was a little store about four blocks down Rue Royal that was still open, and that I should not waste any time as people were buying up everything in sight. I thanked him and power-walked towards the store.

By this time hardly any cars were moving around, so I briskly walked right down the middle of the street. I was going to get some of that food and water or else. When I was about a block away I could see a line of people outside the store. It was just one of those little neighborhood corner stores that looked like it hadn't changed much in the last fifty years. I walked the last few feet and got in line.

There were around two dozen people in line. At least that was how many I could see who were still waiting to get inside the store. I had no idea of the number who were already on the other side of that front door. They all looked to me like they were probably local people, those who had decided to weather the storm in place, and who now decided it was time to get serious about stocking up before Katrina hit. They just had that New Orleans marching-to-my-own-drummer-look about them, that *laissez les bon temps rouler* feeling that I love. I was probably the only out-of-towner in line, and I hoped that wasn't obvious to the others. With the rapidly shifting feelings in the air, that creeping strangeness that the approaching storm was bringing I wasn't sure how local people would feel about an out-of-towner buying up "their" supplies.

Everyone was pretty quiet, which struck me as odd, because I kept expecting some sort of comradeship, you know, the ole "we're all in this together" to break out. However, at that same time, I realized that they were all my competitors for whatever was left in that store. It was an odd mixture of feelings, wanting to make a connection at the same time that I was unconsciously sizing each one of them up to see who posed the biggest challenge.

After waiting fifteen minutes in the sun, I made it inside to the musty, cramped store. There were three small isles and the line went right up the entry aisle, took a left turn at the beverage coolers, and then another left turn right back up the next aisle and headed towards the front of the store. Once it got to the front, it took a sharp right u-turn and headed down the next aisle back the opposite direction. It made one final u-turn up the last aisle and ran straight for the cash register.

As I slowly lined my way through the store, I checked each shelf to see if there was something that I could use. As I passed the first few shelves, I grabbed several granola bars and a container of nuts. The biggest challenge was that I didn't know what was around the corner on the next shelf or the one after that so I had to choose from what was right in front of me even though I might find something better later. I also didn't want to seem "piggish" by buying up everything in sight while there were so many of my "line comrades" breathing down my neck and watching my every move. Simultaneously, I was watching the ones in front of me, seeing what they were getting and if they were going to leave anything for the rest of us. I'd spot something on a shelf a few people ahead and just hope that it would still be there by the time I single-filed my way to it. No pushing, no shoving, just slowly snaking my way towards that six pack of bottled water four people ahead of me.

What to buy, what to buy? How do you shop for a Category 5 hurricane? I had no personal experience to draw on, but I knew I couldn't get anything that required refrigeration and could only get what I could carry. I didn't know how long I'd have to depend on this stuff, so I thought I'd better get too much than too little. At the same time, I didn't want to look panicked by buying too much. I had to keep my cool, or at least look like it. That need to look like I was keeping my cool would rapidly change over the next few days.

SEVEN

TAKING MY SUPPLIES BACK TO THE HOTEL

August 28, 2005. The Late Afternoon Before Katrina.

I t was now around 4 p.m. and I was still snaking my way to the cash register. In addition to the granola bars and nuts, I had a six-pack of bottled water, and six little boxes of raisins. That seemed to be the best pickings and despite what I said earlier about not getting anything that required refrigeration, I was holding a couple of containers of yogurt. I figured that even when the power went off, the mini-bar refrigerator in my room would keep them edible for at least a day.

Of course, the one thing that I really wanted most of all, aside from water, was a flashlight. Even before I got to the store, I knew that would take a minor miracle.

As I inched my way to the checkout counter, I scanned the racks behind it and saw only empty shelves where the flashlights and batteries normally sat. I'll bet had there been any left they would likely have been sitting on those shelves for a couple of years anyway. Nonetheless, facing the reality that I was going to spend a lot of time in the dark over the next few days did leave me with a feeling I can only describe as my own private Richard III moment. What I would have given for a flashlight for my room.

As I mentioned earlier we were all strangely quiet in that line. We weren't really talking nor were we even making much eye contact. When I did make eye contact with one of the others there was no flicker of recognition, no "how's it going" crinkling of the eyes. There was only a furtive look. I think we all felt foolish in a way. You know, we were the "rabbits" who had played too long while the turtles had been steadily accumulating their supplies. It was as if standing in that line was a public admission of laziness or at the very least poor planning so we avoided eye contact out of shame and pure competition.

Finally I reached the goal that I had been fixated on for the last half hour; I was standing in front of the cash register. A young Asian woman took my money while an older man, perhaps her father, stood just behind her watching both every move she made and all of us at the same time. He looked as if he expected trouble and I guess I couldn't blame him. Maybe he'd been through this before. I paid and finally walked past the growing line into the late afternoon air.

On my way back to the hotel, a guy stopped me, just as I had done earlier, and asked where I had gotten my supplies. I directed him down the street and made my way to the hotel. I took the stuff to my room, crammed the yogurt into the mini-bar refrigerator, which was one of those that counted a "sale" when you picked an item up and took it out. I wasn't sure if I had just purchased three Heinekens, two Bud Lights and a couple of bottles of water.

I flipped on the TV to catch the latest on the storm and nothing had changed. It was a Category 5 storm, it wasn't turning away from New Orleans, and it was expected to make landfall the next morning around 6:30 am. I haven't talked much about the anxiety and fear, but I've got to tell you I was afraid. It's the strangest damned thing, waiting for a hurricane. I mean, I'm used to earthquakes which strike with absolutely no warning, but this, this having a couple of days of dread and fear was all new.

I decided to see if I could find someplace to get a late lunch. I thought the chances were slim, but I couldn't just sit in my room stewing. On the elevator ride down, I realized that I had no idea what I was supposed to do when the storm struck nor any idea of what the hotel was prepared to do, so I stopped in the lobby to ask the concierge.

It took me a minute in the crowded lobby, which by now had become a refugee center, but I found her standing next to the concierge desk answering a question. When it was my turn, I asked her what we were supposed to do. "Should we come down to the lobby or a ball room or something when the storm hits?"

"What, do you mean all the guests coming down to the lobby? God I hope not. I don't want all those people down here," she said. I didn't find this very reassuring. The "concierge demeanor," that professional wall that normally separates "guest" from "hotel staff" was cracking. I knew that I was hearing what this woman really felt, completely unedited by whatever "concierge" filter was normally there.

With my sense of "normalcy" just about completely obliterated, I set off into the Quarter looking for a bar or a restaurant where I might find my last meal: my last normal meal.

EIGHT

IN SEARCH OF A FINAL MEAL

August 28, 2005. The Late Afternoon Before Katrina.

It was now around 5 p.m. and I left the hotel in search of a final pre-Katrina-still-got-power meal. I left by the garage exit and crossed to a little pedestrian walkway, Exchange Place, which took me by some small shops, offices, and old empty storefronts. As I began walking down this path, I noticed a small bakery coffee shop with the door open and lights on. Feeling hopeful, I walked in. A distressed looking guy behind the counter was busy, moving trays of pastries out of the display case. When I asked him if he had any coffee, he looked at me and said, "You've got to be kidding. There's a hurricane on its way." I turned around and walked out.

I walked the one block to Bourbon Street, and if you've ever been to New Orleans you know that something is always happening there. Well, today, just twenty-four hours before Katrina, only a few people walked the street, and I couldn't see any store, bar, club nor anything else that was open: nothing.

With each new strange experience, I kept saying to myself "OK, that's weird." It was as if the inner model of what the world is "normally" like was being constantly proven wrong. You know, you have a flight booked and it actually takes off: wrong. The mental and emotional work required to keep up with what was now my new fast changing "normal" was one of the biggest challenges of the whole Katrina experience. The central question for me, and in fact, how well I fared through Katrina, became how quickly I could let go of what I thought was going to happen, accept what was actually happening instead, and deal with it.

I walked a couple of more blocks on Bourbon St. when I noticed a small group of people crowded around the entrance to a bar, all holding and drinking cold beers. I headed straight for them. I wasn't sure if they were still open and if they were, if they had room or food, but I was going to find out.

I maneuvered past the crowd and let my eyes adjust to the low light inside, but I could already see that the bar was open and there was food. Feeling relief, but not knowing if they were still serving, I made my way to a table near the end of the bar and sat down. Nobody paid any attention to me, but I did expect someone to walk up and tell me to leave. No one did. I held my ground.

I sat taking in the place, which was full of people drinking, eating and talking. The TV over the bar was on and, of course, tuned to Katrina coverage. There was a hand-printed sign on the door that said, "The Oceanic Welcomes Hurricane Katrina." I can't tell you how reassuring that sign was, because it was what I expected of New Orleans. Carrying on with life and laughing in the face of danger fit neatly into my inner category of "normal for New Orleans," and that little sign restored a tiny sense of my normalcy.

Finally as the waiter passed my table, he looked back over his shoulder and asked if I'd been helped yet. Hey, I thought, this is normal. "No," I told him. He delivered what looked like Gumbo to another table and came back with a menu and a cloth to wipe off my table. I ordered a big beer and a glass of water. While he was getting those, I checked out the menu and settled on fried calamari and salad. What I was going to eat was much less important than the fact that I was going to eat.

My water and beer arrived shortly and I quickly drank them both. Walking just a couple of blocks in the heat had worn me down. When my food arrived, I dove in and ate everything. I felt like I couldn't get enough food. No, I was scared that I *wouldn't* get enough.

So there I sat in the Oceanic Bar loading up on carbs and protein for what was to come. It wasn't a conscious decision, but my body and soul were switching into survival mode and preparing for the storm in ways that I would only come to appreciate later, much later.

NINE

BACK TO THE HOTEL FOR FINAL PREPARATIONS

August 28, 2005. The Early Evening Before Katrina.

It was now around 6:30 pm. I paid my bill and walked out of the Oceanic, which had become, in that short period of time, a last little island of life before Katrina. I had no idea what life during and after Katrina would be like, but I knew it would be different.

I walked the several blocks back to the Monteleone and entered into a lobby that was bustling with activity aimed at getting the locals into rooms before the storm. I looked back out the glass-front doors and saw a New Orleans Police Department SUV dropping off another half dozen local people, which was something that would continue throughout the evening. The hotel was becoming, quite literally, a safe port in the storm.

I was already wearing my last clean shirt. What to do? Laundry services were not available nor would they be anytime soon and if you've ever spent time in the South in the heat and humidity, you know that it takes only a few minutes outside for sweat to start soaking your clothes. As such, wearing week-old, rolled-up-into-a-wad tee shirts seemed like it was now going to be the new "normal" for me.

I walked towards the elevator and passed the hotel gift shop. Normally I believe that to buy anything in a hotel gift shop is to get ripped off. However, not wanting to gross myself out for the next several days, I parked my reservations at the door and walked in. A young woman greeted me with a nice smile, which helped ease my transition from "judgmental-hotel-gift-shop-boycotter" to "grateful-last-minute-natural-disaster-on-its-way" shopper.

I was determined to minimize the "rip off" factor, so I bought the minimum that I thought I'd need—two tee shirts for $20 each. After all, the storm would hit tomorrow, the Feds would take a day to mobilize and I'd be out by Tuesday at the latest, so two seemed about right. Actually, the shirts were quite nice, one black and one red, with the Hotel Monteleone name and crest embroidered on the front.

Feeling satisfied that I was now ready for the storm from a wardrobe perspective I caught the elevator to my room. On the way up, I wondered when the hotel was going to give "emergency instructions" on what we should do to not only prepare but what we should do during the storm itself. After I walked in, I found a sheet of paper slid under my door. Here is what it basically said.

"Dear Guests:

Please be assured that the The Hotel Monteleone staff is doing all that we can to ensure your safety during this storm.

The Monteleone has been continuously in operation since 1886 and has survived many hurricanes. Numerous local residents come to the Monteleone for safety during hurricanes.

We ask for your full cooperation by observing a few safety measures, should the storm actually hit New Orleans. Please bear with us under these unusual conditions:

1. FILL YOUR BATHTUB WITH COLD WATER (this will be used to flush your commode). You may use your ice bucket to fill the commode with water in order to flush.

2. IN CASE WE EXPERIENCE A POWER FAILURE, EMERGENCY POWER WILL OPERATE IN SELECTED AREAS OF THE HOTEL. WE WILL DELIVER FLASHLIGHTS TO YOUR ROOM FOR EMERGENCY USE. WE ASK THAT YOU DO NOT WANDER AROUND IN AREAS WHERE THE LIGHTS ARE OUT.

3. PLEASE DO NOT USE THE TELEPHONE, EXCEPT IN AN EMERGENCY. PLEASE DIAL DIRECT IF POSSIBLE.

4. KEEP ALL DRAPES CLOSED TO PROTECT YOURSELF FROM FLYING GLASS IN CASE THE WINDOWS MIGHT BREAK. STAY AWAY FROM WINDOWS.

5. PLEASE LET THE TELEPHONE OPERATOR KNOW IF YOU NEED IMMEDIATE ASSISTANCE. IN THAT CASE THE ASSISTANT MANAGER WILL GET IN TOUCH WITH YOU.

6. HOUSEKEEPING SERVICES WILL NOT BE AVAILABLE DURING THIS TIME.

7. FOOD SERVICE WILL BE AVAILABLE ONLY IN LE CAFE. Breakfast (6:30-10:00am), Lunch (11:00am-2:00pm) and Dinner (5:00pm-8:00pm), BUFFET ONLY, NO A LA CARTE SERVICE. BAR SERVICE WILL BE AVAILABLE IN THE CAROUSEL LOUNGE (11:00am-12:00 midnight).

8. IF WE HAVE POWER WE ADVISE YOU STAY TUNED TO CHANNEL 3 OR TO 870 AM ON THE RADIO FOR THE LATEST INFORMATION ON THE STORM,

9. PETS MUST BE ON LEASH WHEN OUTSIDE OF YOUR ROOM. IN ADDITION, YOU'RE RESPONSIBLE FOR CLEANING UP AFTER YOUR PET.

10. CAREFULLY WATCH ALL CHILDREN.

During this difficult period we are doing our very best to be responsive to everyone's needs. We thank you for your patience and understanding.

THE MANAGEMENT

I was glad for the information, but I still didn't know what to do if things didn't go well when the storm hit. Was I supposed to go into the hallway if the windows blew out? Was I to go down to the lobby? If there were no power and no lights, how was I to find my way down? Actually, come to think of it, the concierge's response to my question a little earlier told me that assembling in the lobby was not the plan.

I was glad to know that I would be getting a flashlight after all and wouldn't be completely in the dark. "Man, that's a lot of flashlights to have on hand," I thought. The instructions about not using the phone "EXCEPT IN AN EMERGENCY" struck me as pretty funny, because as I saw it, the whole situation constituted one giant emergency. I pictured using the phone, but having to reassure the hotel staff that this was truly an emergency, not just some excuse to get on the phone and shoot the breeze with my daughter.

Nonetheless, the instructions did help. Feeling a little better knowing that the café and the Carousel Bar would be open, I started to get ready, figuring I'd go down later and check them out.

TEN

MY LAST NIGHT IN CIVILIZED SOCIETY

August 28, 2005. The Evening Before Katrina.

I t was now around 7:30 p.m. For the cross-country trip, I had brought one bag with an extra pair of shorts, half a dozen tee shirts and my shaving kit. I also had an "over the shoulder" briefcase that I used for my computer, some magazines, a book, writing paper, and pens and the like. I started to pack my bag and flipped on the television: no change. It still looked like the "one that we've been dreading." Great. Watching that coverage of the storm increased my anxiety. No, honestly, I was scared, but I wasn't letting my wife know how worried I was.

Being in that room and packing for the storm by myself I was feeling terribly homesick for Kaitlin. We'd just spent the last week together on the road in Little Red or shopping for her apartment and setting up her room. I found myself thinking that this would be easier to go through if she was there with me. But, then again, I thought, it's much better that she's not here in harm's way and, realistically, it will be easier for me just to have to look after myself, so as hard as it was I let go of her in my heart.

As I was just about finished packing, the fire alarm went off, immediately followed by an announcement over the P.A. system that we were to exit the building immediately by the stairs. "Is this some kind of joke?" I said out loud. Great! Here we are, nervous as cats, and it's more likely that somebody pulled the fire alarm than the building actually being on fire, but the alarm kept ringing and the announcement kept playing so I stuck my head out into the hallway to see what was happening. I didn't see or smell any smoke, but people were filing out of their rooms towards the stairway.

This is about the time that I started to have a major regret about changing my room from one on the fourth floor to this one on the fifteenth, the top of the hotel. Dang, why did I have to be so particular?

Surrendering to the moment, I headed for the stairs, and tried to familiarize myself with the layout of the stairwell just in case I might have to run down later in the dark. Fifteen flights down and I was on the sidewalk with the rest of the hotel guests, all of us wondering what the heck was going on. As I had done in the corner market, I searched the faces for some openness, for some commiseration, but none invited contact so I just milled around the crowd: a stranger among strangers.

After fifteen minutes, a staff member announced that it was safe to go back in, so we single-filed-it back into the lobby, crowded around the elevators and took turns going back up to our rooms. I finished packing my little bag and placed it next to the door for a quick escape. I didn't pack my computer briefcase yet as I'd be surfing the web and emailing for the rest of the evening while I still could. After I checked the TV I decided to see what kind of meal service the hotel offered.

When I got down to the Le Cafe the hostess informed me that dining was buffet-style only, just as the emergency notice had said it would be. I don't suppose I was that hungry, but I couldn't pass up the chance for a last good meal. She showed me to a table for two that was in a line of tables with chairs on one side and a long padded bench on the other. I sat down on the bench next to a young couple who were already halfway through their dinner. I again looked for a friendly conversation with a stranger, but everyone seemed to be busy eating or talking to someone else.

I walked over to the buffet and surveyed the food — mashed potatoes, gravy, chicken, fish, green beans, and salad so I picked out a few things and went back and sat down. I finished eating, and went around the corner to the Carousel Bar in the lobby.

If you've ever spent any time in New Orleans, you've probably been to or heard of the Carousel Bar, with the patrons sitting at a circular bar that slowly revolves around the bartender. Adding to its allure is the fact that it has a long and distinguished literary history. Truman Capote used to hang out there and even once claimed that is where he was born. William Faulkner and Tennessee Williams also spent their share of time at the Carousel. It's a well-loved fixture of the city.

I ordered a beer and sat at a small table in the corner by the large front picture window, as all of the carousel seats were taken. The bar was dimly lit and the two televisions suspended from the ceiling were turned to the all-Katrina-all-the-time local news channels. The patrons at the bar were slowly circling the bartender, smoking, drinking, talking loudly and laughing, as predictions of doom flashed on the two television screens. The contrast was so stark that it only added to my now Titanic-sized feelings of alienation and anticipation. If they were all this relaxed about it why was I so concerned?

As I drank my beer, I noticed the small glass oil lamp burning on my table, which couldn't have been larger than about four by four inches. It was one of those candle lamps that bars use to add "atmosphere," but it was now going to be my own personal storm light. I decided that I was going to take it back up to my room, but I needed matches, so I asked the bartender if he had any. I felt pretty guilty for my planned theft, like somehow he'd know what I had in mind and was going to stop me. I think that has something to do with growing up in a home where my mother always said she could read the guilt on my face long before I ever confessed to my crimes. Nevertheless, the bartender turned out not to have that same ability, either that or it was too dark in there for him to get a clear view of my face, so he handed me a small book of matches.

I took the matches and walked back over to my table where I slowly and casually picked up the lamp, tucked it into the side of my body opposite the bartender and walked out. When no alarms went off and no screams of "stop that man" followed me out of the bar, I felt elated, making up for having not found a flashlight to buy earlier in the day.

I caught the elevator back up to my room and set the lamp and matches on the nightstand and practiced finding them with my eyes shut. I undressed, flipped on the television, got my computer out and started surfing the web while I watched storm coverage. The news repeated the same coverage of the last seven hours, so I flipped to the Discovery Channel and watched a soothing "nature" program. I called my wife one last time repeating the facts about how long the hotel had been there and how many storms it had been through. I got off the phone and turned up the air conditioning. I knew we'd lose power, so I was thinking that I'd get the room as cold as possible, so it would stay cooler longer after the electricity went off. Despite the fact that I knew no matter how cool you get a room, once that air conditioner goes off, the New Orleans summer heat would quickly invade and take over.

At about that time I heard a knock, and since I didn't know anyone, I wondered who it could be. I opened the door but no one was there, so I looked around and saw a maintenance worker walking down the hall with a small cardboard box under his arm. He was hanging something on each door. I couldn't tell, but whatever it was, it was pretty small. I looked down at my door handle and there was a tiny, white flashlight hanging on a small key chain. It was one of those plastic flashlights that you have to squeeze to turn on and keep on. I closed the door and went back into my room. "So that's how they managed to have a flashlight for everyone," I thought.

I walked over to the windows to look out at the city lights as if I was taking my last look at the world, as I knew it. I even took three or four pictures to capture New Orleans before the storm even though you couldn't tell if I was in New Orleans or Memphis. I knew it was silly, but I felt a compulsion to do it.

Finally, around midnight, as the wind was picking up and rain sprinkles were starting, I shut down the computer, packed up my brief-case, set it next to my bag by the door, laid out my clothes on the other double bed so they'd be easy to find, flipped off the light, and slipped between the cool sheets in my pitch black room, alone, waiting for Katrina.

Eleven

Katrina Blows Into Town

Monday, August 29, 2005. The Morning of Katrina.

After I got into bed, it took me quite awhile to fall asleep. My thoughts kept racing to the morning: what it was going to be like when the storm hit. I really didn't know if the roof would come off or if flying debris would blow through the hotel. I didn't think the building would come down, but I didn't know. My greatest fear was that the windows would blow out, which seemed pretty likely, so I securely closed the heavy drapes just before I got into bed. If the windows did shatter, I knew I'd escape to the hall, but that's about as far as my plan and the hotel instructions went. All I could do now was wait out the storm, so I did what I did as a kid when I was afraid; I got under the covers, tucked the sides in around my whole body mummy-style, and pulled them up tight around my neck. When that storm hit I was going to be in that bed covered up to my neck in a blanket-cocoon. Man, there must be something primal about that, you know, like being back in the womb or something, but it gave me enough security that I was finally able to fall into a fitful sleep.

I probably woke up at least every half hour listening to the wind and rain grow stronger just on the other side of the quarter-inch thick glass separating me from that storm. Once when I was awake I thought about the story I'd seen on TV of a family who'd decided to ride out a Florida hurricane and how when interviewed after the storm, they explained that they'd had to retreat to the bathtub (the only part of the house still standing) in order to survive. More importantly, they swore they'd never do it again, ever. I remember thinking that they were pretty big idiots, but here I was now, one of those very same idiots with a bathtub full of water that I couldn't even crawl into. I tried to quit thinking and just go back to sleep.

Another time I woke up and thought about all of those hotel bathtubs full of water and worried that the sheer weight could bring down the building. Had anyone done the calculations on that? When the Golden Gate Bridge turned fifty years old they closed the roadway to cars one early Sunday morning and let people walk out onto the bridge. It was wall to wall people, so many in fact, that the roadway, which normally has an upward curve, completely flattened out. The weight of the people was more than any collection of vehicles and nobody had anticipated that. It was only afterwards that the bridge engineers got concerned when they looked at the photographs. I was one of those people on the bridge and I've visualized many times two hundred thousand of us crashing into the water. If the bridge engineers had missed that I didn't have much faith that the hotel building engineers had calculated the weight and impact of the bath water. I've got to go back to sleep, I kept thinking.

When awake, I could hear the sheets of rain pounding on the windows. As I told you, we'd been warned to stay away from the windows, so I was leery even to look out. I had repeatedly fallen asleep and woken up to find myself under the covers, completely in the dark and alone, as the building shook and swayed.

I finally got out of bed around 6:30 a.m. and looked out the window. I carefully pulled the heavy drapes open just enough to see out. The wind was howling, and the rain was being blown completely sideways. There was a heavy dark cloud cover and the combination of the clouds, the rain and wind made it difficult to see beyond a couple dozen feet. I felt like I was breaking a rule by standing there; worse, I imagined that the next big gust would take the windows out and me with them.

The wind gusts had been so strong and in so many different directions, including up, that rainwater had been driven into the seams in the window casings, so the inside of the drapes and the carpet were soaking wet and water had pooled on the window ledges. I laid some towels on the ledges.

I didn't know for sure, but it looked like I had made it through the worst of the storm. I stuck my head out into the hallway to see if anyone was up and about, and found it completely empty and dark. I could hear no other sound than the storm and the creaking of that old building. I didn't know how much more was to come, so I decided to get back in bed. I had no electricity and I was wiped out from all of the adrenalin not just from the previous night, but also from the several days leading up to the hurricane. Before drifting back into intermittent sleep, I was relieved that the hard part was over.

TWELVE

KATRINA PEAKS AND MOVES ON

Monday, August 29, 2005. Katrina Passes
Through New Orleans.

I got back up around 10:15 a.m. and went to the windows. I parted
the heavy drapes and could see over the city for maybe a mile,
which lay under a heavy, grey cloud layer. Katrina was still going with
rain and wind gusts, but I could tell we were on the backside of the
storm. I don't know what I expected, but I couldn't see any activity
on the streets and it seemed only the roof of a building about a block
and a half away was damaged. I thought there would be more visible
damage, but this early look revealed a fundamental truth about the
character of Katrina. Each person's experience of the hurricane in
New Orleans was centered on the relatively small part of the city in
which they found themselves, making for thousands of vastly different
stories of what it was like during Katrina.

As it happened, I was in the French Quarter, which didn't flood
for the most part due to its unique geography. The Quarter lies next
to the Mississippi River, one of the high points of the city, with the
land sloping down and away, meaning that the closer one was to the
river, at least in the Quarter and the Garden District, the less likely

one was to be flooded. From my perspective, Katrina hadn't caused much damage.

After lingering at the window, I figured this would be a day to hang out, survey the damage, see what was working and what wasn't, and generally get a sense of what a Category 5 storm can do. I knew we wouldn't be "rescued" on the first day of the storm, but by Tuesday, I fully expected that the government and disaster groups like the Red Cross would take over and begin rescue, recovery, and evacuation. That is the way it had always happened before.

With no power and the cloud cover, it was still fairly dark in the room. I got dressed, brushed my teeth in the dark and headed out the door to the elevator, just a few steps out of my door. There was water leaking from the hallway ceiling just in front of the elevators and someone had moved the large floor ashtray, (the kind that hotels use sand in and rake to try to make them look like Zen gardens), into the middle of the hall. I think there were six elevators total in the hotel and two were working on generator power. The hallway lights were also working on the generator, although in a somewhat reduced state, much like my own.

Two of the three sets of double glass doors at the front lobby had been boarded up with plywood, and sand bags had been placed around the bottom, leaving only the one door open. Those doors and the dim lighting gave the formerly elegant lobby the look and feel of something out of *Long Day's Journey Into Night*.

I walked over to the Carousel Bar and it was taped off with yellow "caution" tape. I could see that one of the picture windows was blown out and the rain and wind were whipping and drenching the bar as I stood there. Still, it hadn't suffered any real, lasting damage. Clearly, the Carousel would not be open from 11 a.m. to midnight.

I wandered over to find the concierge so I could ask about breakfast. The emergency instruction sheet had stated that buffet style food would be served in Le Cafe, however, the doors were closed and the restaurant was dark. I found the concierge and she told me that the meal would actually be served in a ballroom upstairs on the mezzanine so I decided to go up and take a look.

I've talked about layers of normal "civilized" society being stripped away by Katrina. Well, this morning, it was beginning to dawn on me that as layers of civilization were being removed, layers of Katrina were taking their place. In other words, it wasn't just that the normal civilized society of early 21st Century America was being stripped away leaving a vacuum, but rather, the new and unaccustomed experiences that Katrina brought were hitting us, layer by layer.

I found the mezzanine stairs and as I climbed, I could hear the buzz of people talking and milling about. I followed the noise around the corner and down the dim hallway until I came to a "T" intersection where the ballrooms were located. There was a ballroom to my left with a large knot of people gathered around the door and a long line of people stretching away from the door. Within these tangles there was a definite sense of competition for whatever food was in that ballroom.

It looked to me like most of these folks were the locals that had come to the hotel for refuge. Why is it important to note that? Well, one layer of strangeness that Katrina brought was throwing you into extraordinary situations and out of your normal life. As such, I began to experience a mixture of feelings and fears, which I didn't normally encounter. The result was that you are truly not "yourself." In other words, not only are the situations you now find yourself in strange, but you've also become a stranger to yourself. For me then, there was the struggle to adapt to the changed outer world at the same time that I was struggling to cope with the strange inner world being stirred up inside me. I found myself coping with an onslaught of strong feelings that included competition, territoriality, threat, claustrophobia, and alienation just to name a few.

Here's what I mean. As I surveyed that scene of mass confusion, I became conscious that I was the only white guy amidst the several hundred on-edge people crowded in that stuffy and dark hallway This was a new and foreign experience. I really wasn't sure which way to turn.

Another ballroom door stood just to the right, but the snaking line blocked the entrance. I wanted to stick my head in to find anyone in charge and see what the heck was going on, but I was reluctant, really a bit scared, to try to squeeze through that line, and I wasn't getting any green lights from the folks in line either. I was also feeling quite territorial and was being rocked, full force, by thoughts like "well I'm a paid guest and these folks are eating all the food and I can't even get through the damned line to get to the dining room."

Since I grew up with three brothers, I'm a pretty competitive person and I usually think ahead, as far as looking out for my family and myself. Whenever I go to a conference where lunch is served, I pick a table near the front, but close to the food so I have the inside track on lunch. With those three brothers, I learned very fast that I had to jockey for position if I didn't want to end up eating the chicken wing instead of the breast.

Finally, I moved. I politely excused myself and stepped through the line into the second set of ballroom doors, which, as it turns out, led to the very same ballroom that everyone was lined up for. There were people setting up a chow line so I walked over to ask what the drill was. One of the ladies asked me if I was a hotel guest and I told her I was. "Oh, well then, there's another dining room for hotel guests in the ballroom next door." I thanked her, walked back out into the hallway and cut back through the line to get out.

Well, finally, I now not only knew what to do, which was comfort in itself, but my sense of fairness was assuaged and my competitive instincts taken down a notch by learning that the hotel guests were still being treated like guests and not being thrown into one big pot of desperate people in that hotel. I walked the few steps to the next ballroom door, once again excused my way across the line and entered the ballroom set up for food service for hotel guests, ready for breakfast.

Thirteen

My First Meal After Katrina

Monday, August 29, 2005. Late Morning of the Storm.

By the time I'd made my way into that ballroom, it was late morning. As I opened the door, I found a scene similar to the one in the other ballroom: a cafeteria-style line was set up with four ladies, who worked in the hotel, dishing up portions of food. The lights were dim, the room was stuffy and there were a dozen round tables set up for us to sit at once we'd gotten our allotted food. As I stood there, I thought about how many elegant balls and functions had been held in that old ballroom over the hundred and twenty-nine year history of the hotel and how different it looked now.

I got behind four other guests, picked up my plate and silverware and started down the line. Each lady would plop a big ole dollop of whatever they had onto my plate. First, I got the big spoonful of hotel-style-scrambled-eggs. Next came the helping of Southern-style-one-big-sticky-mashed-potato-like-mound-of-grits. Finally, there came slices of bacon cut so thin I could actually see through, followed by two slices of white bread toast. At the end of the line was a big container of water and one of apple juice, both room temperature.

I poured myself a glass of juice and turned to find a place to sit and as I did one of the serving ladies called out, "Don't you want some butter for your grits, Darlin?" I thought about it for a second and, even though I grew up in the South we weren't the grits eating kind of family, but decided, what the heck, it was more food, so I said yes and walked back over to where she was holding out a mass of butter on the end of her long stainless steel serving spoon. I held my plate mid-air and she expertly aimed and topped that white pile of country goodness with a golden crown. Man oh man!

I turned and surveyed the room to find a spot. Now I'm the kind of person that is always careful about selecting where I'm going to sit in a public dining room even under normal life circumstances, but now I really wanted to make the right choice. I didn't want to intrude, nor did I want to sit by myself, and as you know, I had been looking for some kind of connection with others. Some tables held people already in conversations and looked like they knew each other, so I passed on them. As I slowly walked I looked for some invitation, some eye contact, but got none so I kept moving.

I got towards the back of the room where there were several empty tables, and a couple was sitting at one of them. The man, in his mid-forties, balding with a beard and glasses, looked at me and made eye contact, which was just enough invitation for me, so I sat down. The woman, who also looked to be in her mid-forties, had long dark curly hair and was wearing a fanny pack over her khaki shorts. We started that my-name-is, where-are-you-from, and what's-your-story conversation. It turns out that they too were from the San Francisco Bay Area, were software developers, and were in New Orleans for a developers convention. Well now, I thought, Bay Area people. Maybe I could hang out with them for a while for even though I wasn't getting any overwhelming "connection" vibe what I was getting seemed enough.

As we ate our meal and continued with the small talk, I wanted to connect with them on a deeper level and talk about how strange and disorienting the whole experience had been thus far; the waiting for the storm, the great weather prior to the hurricane, the "party on" attitude in the days prior, becoming a virtual prisoner in New Orleans, and the sudden change in atmosphere from a four-star-luxury hotel to a virtual war zone of tension and competition for food brought about by the great influx of so many local people from the neighborhoods. Things were going along fine until I mentioned that last point about the hotel and the mix of people there now. I was looking at the man, and I remember his face going completely blank at that moment. I glanced over at the woman, and her face was blank as well. I don't know what they thought I was trying to say, but I felt like they had taken me the wrong way. I imagined they took my comment to be born out of an elitist or prejudiced attitude, which it wasn't. I was desperately trying to ground my own disorientation by talking with others who might be having a similar experience. I took a risk to take the conversation to a deeper level and discuss my real feelings, and I hit a brick wall. What to do, what to do? There was some awkward silence, a few more superficial comments about the weather, and I excused myself from the table. As I walked over to drop off my dirty dishes, I knew that any chance of hanging out with them was gone. Well, you may say I was reading more into it and stuff, but at that moment I was feeling pretty stressed and alienated, a condition that would only deepen.

I made my way back out into the hallway, through the mass of people and downstairs. I decided to go out to the garage and see what was happening on the weather front. A long hallway led through a sliding glass door into the garage.

When I got to the garage, nearly thirty people stood just inside the door watching the rain and wind blow down the street. If you didn't know that this was the tail end of a hurricane you would have thought it a bad rainstorm. I stood there for maybe half an hour as we all just wanted to get an up-close look at the storm that had already changed the last several days of our lives.

FOURTEEN

THE LOOTING STARTS

Monday, August 29, 2005. Late Afternoon
on the Day of the Storm.

A fter standing and watching the tail end of the storm I went back
to my room to get ready for my first excursion. Despite my air
conditioning blast, the room was heating up. After the long darkness
of the night before, I welcomed the open curtains and sunlight. Those
old windows once opened, but had been painted shut a long time ago,
so getting any fresh air was out of the question.

Sensing that the storm's impact might be much worse than I
could see, I called Southwest and changed my flight from Tuesday
to Wednesday. I called my wife to tell her my flight plans and let her
know that I was all right. It was now late afternoon, the rain and wind
had stopped, and the cloud cover was still there, but with occasional
breaks.

I grabbed my wallet and camera, caught the elevator downstairs,
and headed out the front door onto Rue Royal. It's only about a quarter block to the next cross street and on that corner was the Walgreens
drug store in which I had bought my sunglasses. As I approached the

intersection, I heard a large crowd cheering. What was happening? When I got into the intersection I got my answer; looters were walking out of Walgreens with double armfuls of goods and as each one emerged from the store, a cheer went up.

I couldn't believe what I was seeing. The looting was shocking enough, but to have people standing around cheering was even more disturbing. Where was I, how could this be happening? Had people completely lost their minds? I stood there not knowing what to do, but feeling I had to do something. I could see some police officers at the corner of Royal and Canal Street, so I decided to alert them. I've got to tell you, it was so weird, going for help, against the grain of the crowd, and feeling like a spoilsport.

As I was making my way down the street, I passed two New Orleans Sheriff's deputies who were walking toward the Walgreens. I turned to see how they would handle the situation, and to my astonishment, they walked right past that Walgreens, without even so much as looking over.

Dismayed, I continued towards the police officers at the corner. When I got about three quarters of the way there, two of them turned and headed in my direction towards the Walgreens, so I waited for them to pass, then trailed along to see if they were going to take any action. They headed right for the Walgreens and as they got near the front door, a couple of looters came out. One officer stood watch facing the crowd while the other one calmly confronted the looters, turned them around, sent them right back into the store, and then slid the glass doors shut. This sealed all of the looters in an instant holding cell.

The looters had grabbed whatever they could and were carrying bags of stuff, some even pushing shopping carts full of electronics, cameras, film, sunglasses, water, food, and DVD's among other items. People weren't desperate for food and water yet, so this seemed to me to be a target of opportunity. In fact, a teenage boy ran by and asked someone near me, "Where's the Shoe Locker store?" I don't know where the first incident of looting started, but it was like the castle wall had been breached once those first few stores went down and now it was open season for looters.

In the days that followed I tried to find a reasonable explanation for that scene, to see it as the corrosive impact of poverty, of people feeling deprived by society and, therefore, entitled to take what they could given the opportunity. However, that moment signaled that Katrina was bringing more than I bargained for. The American society I knew was quickly coming apart at the seams.

FIFTEEN

MY FIRST LOOK AROUND AFTER THE STORM

Monday, August 29, 2005. Later Afternoon
on the Day of the Storm.

Watching that looting made me realize that the people who adjust the fastest to the changing reality around them are the ones who have the highest chances of survival. It's like you get a picture, a "mental frame," in your mind of your reality that usually matches the outer reality. For example, my mental frame on the Friday before the storm was that I'd just gotten to the end of my father-daughter road trip cross-country and would hang out for a couple days. When that all changed on Saturday, it took me a little while to adjust my new reality, in fact, to my captivity in New Orleans. You go through that, "this isn't supposed to be happening" mental phase in which you keep comparing what you thought was going to happen to what's really happening and you keep trying to fit the two together. For that period, until you get in tune with the new reality, you are essentially impaired, "one click" away from reality, meaning it takes you longer to process information, to make decisions, and most importantly, to make the right decisions. I was fast learning that the ability to shift quickly to embrace a changed circumstance or a dashed expectation is one of the qualities that a good leader possesses, and one that may keep you alive.

Standing in the intersection in front of that Walgreens, which had now been transformed into a "looter's holding cell," I was still stunned by what I had just witnessed. The mood of the crowd was one of disappointment, but with a barely suppressed thread of hostility running through it as the police ended the fun. So I decided it was time to move on.

I walked the short block down to Bourbon Street and it was surreal to see the street with all of the stores and clubs shut and with just a few small wandering groups of people. I'd only been there when the street was really cooking. To walk down Bourbon Street at night, just about any night, is to take a trip into another world. I mean, with the street closed off to cars, with all of the people crowding the street with drinks in hand, with the music and cigarette smoke billowing out of the bars, with the smell of sweat, perfume and garbage all mixed together, with the glittery tourist shops and their carnival masks, pink wigs, tee shirts, and feather boas you might as well be in a different country, a much more exotic one than the United States that I know.

I couldn't really get my bearings. There was very little damage from the storm aside from the occasional sign blown down or a tree titling sideways. We were a strange looking bunch, mostly out-of-towners like myself, who had emerged from the downtown hotels. We were just strolling, taking in the famous Bourbon Street after the big storm. I wanted to walk up and stop someone, anyone, and say, "Can you believe this? Isn't this weird?" to validate my current take on reality, which was getting quite slippery. I don't mean that I was going nuts or anything like that, but that reality itself was shifting pretty quickly and I was running as fast as I could to keep up, and I was falling behind.

I decided to head over to Jackson Square and see what was happening there. Remember, this was not the Hurricane Katrina story as you've come to know it just quite yet. I had no knowledge of any flooding or levee breaks and as far as we knew, we had just come through a Category 5 storm relatively unscathed. So as I walked, I saw little damage. I was feeling pretty lucky and looking forward to going home the next day or so.

When I got to Jackson Square, I first noticed the row of banana trees that lined the fence on the inside of the Square. Banana leaves are large and grow out of the top of the tree trunk, and the trunks of these trees were just about as high as the fence. The result was that the leafy tops of the trees had all been blown forward over the fence. They looked like bright green curtains that had been draped over the fence in some sort of Christo project.

It was now twilight, and I crossed Jackson Square to see the famous Cafe du Monde, which has been around in one form or another since 1862. It's open twenty-four hours a day, seven days a week, except for Christmas and "on the day an occasional Hurricane passes too close to New Orleans," according to their website. I think they thought that was cute, but today it was too real to be funny. The cafe has one of those red Spanish tile roofs, and several of the tiles now lay shattered into small pieces on the sidewalk. I had spent good times there with Kaitlin having chicory-laced cafe au lait and beignets so I, like many people, have an emotional attachment to the now darkened place.

I decided I'd pick up one of those broken tiles as a souvenir for Kaitlin, you know, your chance to own a piece of history, a piece of Cafe du Monde blown off by Hurricane Katrina. It took awhile to select a piece with a nice shape, but not too heavy as I'd have to carry it. I finally settled on a couple of pieces that, despite being small, were still pretty heavy due to the thickness of the tile.

I put them in my camera case and headed up the levee to what's called the "Moon Walk," or the walking path that runs along the top of the levee beside the Mississippi River. The river was quiet as I walked down the path and finally settled into a bench overlooking the water. By now it was near sunset, and over my right shoulder the sky was turning from gray to pink.

As I was sitting there a small bird, probably a sparrow flew down and landed on the walkway in front of me. He looked up at me as if to say, "Man, can you believe what just happened?" It was either that or "Dude, I'm starving!" Regardless, I was touched by that little bird and I asked him out loud, "Well how did you get through the storm? Where did you stay that got you out of that killer wind?" He just looked at me, but I finally felt a bond with another living creature, one who had gone through Katrina, like me, and come out the other side. We sat there for maybe five minutes, neither of us wanting to strike out on our own again. I'd been looking for connection in all of the people around me and hadn't found it, yet here now sitting on that bench with that little bird looking up at me I finally had.

Sixteen

The Katrina Plot Thickens

Monday, August 29, 2005. Evening on the Day of the Storm.

After sitting by the river with my bird buddy, I decided to walk the seven-blocks back to the hotel. As I got up I saw a huge line of dark green pick-up trucks, some pulling aluminum fishing boats, driving by. It was hard to make out the insignia, but I finally could see that they were all Louisiana Wildlife and Fisheries trucks. There must have been two dozen of them headed away from downtown. I had no idea what they were doing. I thought it was a bit strange to see so many from that agency now, but figured they were here to help with rescue.

After they passed, I headed for the hotel. Remember how I had seen both New Orleans Police officers and Sheriffs Deputies on foot earlier in the day? Well, walking back alone now through the darkened Quarter, I didn't see a single one. However, twice on my walk I saw two New Orleans Police cars speeding by with blue police lights flashing. With the only police presence being the occasional cruiser, and after my earlier encounter with the looters and their supporters, all my senses were on high alert; my scanners were working the environment around me double time. It's funny how quickly you can slip into a self-protective mode.

When I got back to the hotel lobby, one of the first things I overheard was that a levee or levees had broken and the city was flooding. I stopped and asked these people what they knew. They said they hadn't seen any flooding, but had heard that eight feet of water was headed our way as we spoke. Suddenly all of those Wildlife & Fisheries trucks with their aluminum boats started to make more sense. I asked what we were supposed to do and nobody seemed to know. Since no one else seemed worried about the wall of water headed our way and since the hotel was taking no specific action, I thought I'd take a wait and see attitude.

I decided to get some dinner and when I climbed the mezzanine stairs, I was greeted by the same mass of people. Before crossing what seemed like a picket line, I headed for the bathroom, as I hadn't had an opportunity to make a stop for half a day.

There was one public restroom across from the ballroom, but it had no light. The hallway was lit by emergency generator lights, but none of that light penetrated the bathroom. I was reluctant to walk into that darkness, because I was wearing a pair of Mexican sandals, which meant my feet were exposed to whatever I might step in.

It had only been one day with no power or water, but the bathroom already smelled awfully bad. I willed my way inside and tried to let my eyes adjust, but it was so dark there was no light to adjust to. So I started very slowly, step by step, like Frankenstein, with my arms stretched wide out in front of me feeling for whatever might be in my path. I thought I was heading towards the wall that the urinals were on, but I wasn't quite sure so I kept slowly inching my way forward. Just about the time my fingers touched a cold tile, I took one more step forward and my right foot landed in about four inches of mystery liquid, but I had a pretty good idea what it was since the toilets were now plugged up and overflowing.

I steeled myself and felt down the wall. I could feel a lever, then the top of what I believed to be the urinal, so I took one more step and took care of business. There was nowhere to wash my foot, as there was no running water. I had seen some rainwater pooled along the curb in front of the hotel earlier in the day so I headed back down stairs and out the front doors to the street, where, sure enough there was about four inches of water up to the curb, now dirty with trash that had been blown around by the storm. I rushed over and put my right, sandaled foot into that water and moved it rapidly back and forth a couple of times. A woman, who happened to be walking by, looked over and said, "Ooouu, you don't know where that water has been."

"Lady if you knew where my foot has been you'd understand," I said.

Now that I had done what I could to clean my feet, I headed back to the ballroom. The salad lady gave me a helping, followed by a big dollop of white rice, and a couple of slices of white bread. I saw the software developers sitting by themselves in the back so I went the other way. No reason to engage in more awkward conversation.

I wanted to spend as little time as possible at my unoccupied table since the dining hall was dim, hot and stuffy. I chased the salad, gummy rice, and doughy bread down with lukewarm water. I collected my plate and utensils, and deposited them in the clean up area.

I cruised back to the lobby to check the eight feet of water rumor and there was no update, so I figured we were safe for the moment. Although I was now ensconced high and dry on the fifteenth floor, that would be little consolation if the emergency generator failed and I faced fifteen flights of stairs.

Satisfied that we weren't all immediately about to drown, I took the elevator to my even hotter, stuffier room. The hotel had no coffee, nor was there any place else to get any so after a full twenty-four hours, I had a throbbing caffeine-withdrawal headache.

I found my tiny flashlight, made my way to the phone and called my wife, who turned out to be my main source of information. I could only follow an eight-block radius of my hotel and since that was all in the Quarter, I could hardly see any flooding. However, she was glued to the coverage of the storm's aftermath, which focused on areas that sustained the most damage. In addition, the news was picking up the stories of looting, shootings and other acts of lawlessness, so my wife was shook up when I called her. She was desperately trying to find a way to get me out of there, and I assured her that I was confident that the authorities would come in to start evacuating us the next day.

Seventeen

Closing Out the First Day of the Storm

Monday, August 29, 2005. Late Evening the Day of the Storm.

Being in the dark, except for my tiny squeeze flashlight, there wasn't much to do except to make sure I had everything I needed nearby. I set my stolen lamp on my nightstand and ran a match down the side of the box, but nothing happened. I struck it three or four more times and still nothing, so I decided to try another. Again, nothing happened except for the head of the match wearing off. I tried several more times until I finally accepted that the matches were too damp. The rainwater that had blown in the windows and soaked the carpet and drapes had given the whole room a damp, but hot feel.

I nearly cried. I had been keeping the thought of that little lamp in the back of my mind like some sort of prized safety valve and now my plan had failed. There is a saying that I think dates from World War I that goes something like "Trust in the Lord, but keep your powder dry." Well, I wasn't doing too well at either one just then.

I had to get my mind off of the disappointment of the lamp, and I had noticed a maid's closet just across the hall so I decided to see if there were matches or other supplies that I could use. I grabbed my squeeze light, crossed the hall and pushed the door open. I was met by a large laundry cart partly blocking the door. It looked as if it had been quickly shoved into the room. I pushed past it and opened a cabinet that was normally locked, and to my surprise sitting there on the shelf was a gorgeous bottle of red wine.

Now, you've got to understand that at this point the mentality of "scarcity" was already deeply rooted. It was clear that if you didn't have what you needed you weren't going to get it. So as I stood there in front of that wine I was torn. If I took it, wasn't I just like the looters? On the other hand, it seemed kind of dumb to, out of some high-minded principle, deny myself something that could be a great source of comfort. This was the second "moral" decision facing me after my encounter earlier with the looters. After thinking it through I decided that I would "liberate" the wine. After all, I could always tell the hotel and pay them for it later. I grabbed the wine along with some extra towels and rolls of toilet paper and crossed back to my room.

When I got back, I started to look around for a corkscrew or bottle opener of some sort. It was no easy task with that tiny light, but I did a pretty good search and turned up nothing. Just then I remembered that I had bought a pocket knife, a kind of Swiss Army knife, at one of the wineries near our home in Healdsburg, CA. and it had a tiny corkscrew in addition to all the other jazzed up stuff. Where was it? Talk about ironies, but I had given it to Kaitlin before she left for Houston on Saturday both because I thought she might need it, and I only had carry on bags for my flight home and so couldn't have taken it.

I set the wine bottle aside, snacked on one of my granola bars, and drank some of my water, both of which I had started rationing. Since the story of Katrina was evolving so rapidly, I now had no idea how long I'd need to depend on my own food and water, nor how long the hotel's supply would last.

From phone calls with my wife and my brothers, I had discovered that major flooding, looting, and lawlessness had broken out; in fact, sounds of gunshots were being reported. It was beginning to look like the greatest danger now lay in other people, rather the forces of nature. It was as if Katrina had wiped out the normal rules of society, and people were acting on their basest impulses. Knock out society's rules, couple it with an overwhelmed police force that had no plan to handle a crisis of this magnitude, and we were in chaos.

Settling in for the night, I locked the door securely. I might have gotten a little air circulation with the door open, but I wasn't going to take any chances. I brushed my teeth with a tiny bit of water, took my contacts out and lay down on the bed. My mind raced over the events of the day and what the next day might bring. I was hoping against hope that when I woke up in the morning I'd find the city crawling with National Guard troops and Red Cross workers. I fell into a sweaty, light sleep.

Eighteen

Tuesday, August 20, 2005. Waking up to Chaos.

I woke up to realize that not only had the National Guard not come but that the city of New Orleans had now been sealed off to anyone other than police, officials, and the press. So now there was no getting out and no getting in.

My wife was getting more panicked by the lawlessness shown on television and was calling anyone she could think of to try and get me out. My brother, Brian, who lives in Arkansas was ready to drive the eight hours to pick me up anytime. However, any kind of private rescue was now impossible. I reassured her that the area right around the hotel seemed to be fairly safe. At least I hadn't heard any gunfire. I was now totally dependent on the authority figures in New Orleans for escape.

Since this was all happening while I was still in bed, I decided to get up, get breakfast and take another look around. I brushed my teeth and tried to hospital-sponge-bath enough to keep myself somewhat decent. I already was not smelling like a rose and neither were any of the other guests. In addition, the room was musty from the wet carpet and drapes.

71

From my window, I could see a cemetery. Since they can't bury people underground due to the high water table in New Orleans, it was easy to see that most of the tombs were a little over half submerged. On the street next to the cemetery the water was almost up to the tops of the car doors. I made a mental note of how high the water was so that I could check its progress later.

I thought about the scene before me. The floodwaters had overtaken this one cemetery near the hotel, which meant that the water had likely flooded practically every cemetery around New Orleans. It was likely that most of those caskets had been breached, so that in addition to the gas, oil, garbage and everything else that the floodwater contained, it also now included residue from the cemeteries. Add to that the storm victims, whose bodies were still in the water, and I got a pretty good idea of how toxic and putrid that storm water was.

Before leaving the room I decided to change my flight. After changing it twice already, I was now scheduled to fly out the next day, Wednesday, around 5:50 p.m. but it didn't look like that was going to happen. Reaching Southwest and still optimistic, I booked my flight for Thursday, giving the "authorities" one more day. Since Southwest took the reservation, I hung up feeling I had a plan.

I grabbed my camera, a bottle of water, a handful of nuts and headed for the elevator. In the dim lobby, which reeked of sweat and overflowing toilets, I looked for any reliable information. I made my way over to the front desk and there was a short line of un-bathed people, like me, wanting to know when help would arrive. Three hotel staff members stood behind the desk trying to answer. When I reached the front of the line, the clerk told me that the hotel management was working as diligently as they could to get us out. She also told me that all of the "neighbors," who had come to the hotel for refuge were being moved out to the convention center. Although I was glad the locals had a place to be safe from the storm, I was also relieved to hear they were leaving, as the sense of competition for the scarce resources had taken a quantum leap forward.

The staff stayed in the hotel during and after Katrina and suffered the same conditions we did. However, they had the extra burden of taking care of us. Wearing civilian clothes now, it was hard to pick them out unless they were standing behind a counter. Most maintained their composure and did their jobs in an admirable fashion.

Oh, one more thing I asked the desk clerk; did they have a corkscrew. The clerk's five-minute search produced nothing, so I thanked her and walked towards the still closed Carousel Bar. The shattered picture window was now boarded over with a very large sheet of plywood.

I braced myself for the impervious chow line. This morning we only had grits, butter, white toast, and lukewarm water. I got my food and passed the two software developers (who seemed not to notice me) to an empty table on the other side of the room. Here I was avoiding people, even though we should have bonded by our mutual need to escape from this weird existence.

I stirred some butter around my grits to try to flavor them and took a bite. Now, I don't know if you've ever eaten grits, but I never developed a taste for them. Even with the butter they tasted like nothing, absolutely nothing. I couldn't even taste the butter. It was as if the combination of grits and butter canceled each other out.

Concluding that was all the grits I could take, I decided to head outside. I grabbed my things and walked towards the hotel garage exit. In this hallway, someone had let their dog poop right on the old carpet and had just left it there.

In these few days, I had to reconcile a plethora of sights—looting, flooding, shootings, angry crowds, the whole city dark with no power or water, tense and anxious food lines, and now dogs pooping in the hallways of a grand old hotel, one that had withstood many storms for the past hundred and twenty-nine years. These experiences were piling up in my brain, leaving me with one overriding feeling in the center of my heart, one that I was struggling to contain; *I just wanted to go home.*

Nineteen

Out Into the Heat

Tuesday, August 30, 2005. Mid-day.

I 've mentioned how hot and stuffy the hotel had become, but that was nothing compared with the wall of heat that greeted me outside. I was looking for a spot, a place where I could sit down away from the craziness at the hotel and away from other people. I couldn't get it in my room, because it was just too damned hot.

No, you don't understand. It was really hot. It's quite impossible to convey just how hot it was. The heat was one of the most underappreciated elements of the entire Katrina story, one that caused massive suffering. New Orleans in the summer is normally hot and humid, but the weather that followed Katrina had a nasty, punishing edge to it. The fact that over two-thirds of the city was covered in water only made it that much more humid. The mass and weight of the heat pressed against my face and prevented me from getting any air. It was alive, holding me in a heat cocoon and there was no escape.

I left the garage, took the small pedestrian walkway to the other end, and walked past a small cafe to see what was happening at the police station next door. About a dozen police cars were parked outside, and a generator in the courtyard provided power to the station. A couple of officers were grilling burgers on an outdoor grill and as I walked past one of them grabbed a couple and whisked them into the station. They paid no notice to me. Well, I thought, it looks like these guys are taking care of themselves pretty well. I know I probably shouldn't have begrudged them these comforts, but something struck me as odd; they were taking care of themselves while the rest of the city was in dire need.

I walked back to the cafe and noticed two wire-mesh tables turned upside down, and half a dozen chairs stacked two by two. I could imagine people sitting and enjoying a cool drink and nice lunch, but instead dead leaves littered the ground. A bicycle cable locked the tables and chairs together. No one was around but me, so I decided this was as good a spot as any to stake a claim. I couldn't un-stack the chairs because of the cables, so I pushed the table over next to the two chairs stacked closest and sat down. Since we couldn't leave New Orleans, there was nothing to do but wait for help to arrive.

The book I had brought was titled *Mornings on Horseback*, a biography of Teddy Roosevelt by David McCullough. I wanted to forget about my situation, so my plan was to dive into the world of TR. By now, that feeling of *I want to go home now* was all consuming, as was the heat. As much as I tried to get completely absorbed into the world of late 19th century New York that TR inhabited, time was crawling by. I can now see why a library and books are so important to people in prison.

The breakdown of society was particularly overwhelming, because the situation was dangerous, not just uncomfortable. My wife relayed stories of rapes, murders and muggings at the Superdome and the convention center along with reports of random looting and shooting. When I met someone walking up the street, I didn't know if they were going to pass on by or knock me in the head and rob me. Think about it. When you can't count on this most normal of expectations, you're really in completely new territory. So just at the same time that I needed other people to get me through, my guard was way up.

Across from where I was sitting was an antique store, and just behind that was a door that led to an apartment upstairs. After I'd been sitting there for a couple of hours, long enough to feel some sense of security, that stairway door opened and out stepped an unshaven man, in his late sixties, wearing khaki shorts, tennis shoes, a dirty tee shirt and ball cap. He stood there taking in the whole scene. "Oh no," I thought, "I hope he doesn't come over here," but sure enough, he walked straight to me. He motioned to the two chairs stacked up on the other end of the line, and asked if I minded if he sat down. I told him to go ahead, and he plopped down.

As much as I had been looking for a connection with others, I was trying to escape into my book and the old man was bringing me right back, trapping me in the heat. He wanted to talk. He said something about how hot it was and how he had chosen to stay in his apartment during the storm. I listened politely, but I was giving him "I'm not interested" vibes. I would quickly look down at my book each time he stopped talking. Try as I might, he wasn't getting the message and kept on talking. Then he pulled a pack of cigarettes out of his pocket and asked if I minded. I lied, "No."

I have never smoked, except for a month following the break-up of a relationship in the late seventies. If I'm sitting near someone who is smoking I'll get up and move because I don't like the smell. Well, here I was downwind with a hundred pounds of smoke-filled heat pressure on my face, and I was growing livid inside. The old man and his need to talk and his smoke were taking over my refuge. I turned, ever so slightly away from him, hoping that he'd get the message.

I know the old man was lonely and probably responding to the same need for connection as I had been, but I was in a different phase now, a self-protective mode, and he was an intruder. It may sound hard, but it gets back to what I said about not being yourself in a strange situation like Katrina. Call this my Katrina-induced-hyper-protective-mode.

Just when I couldn't take it any longer, the old man excused himself and walked back over to the open door to his stairway, stepped in and closed it behind him. I could feel all of the muscles in my body start to un-clench. In addition to no bath and profuse sweating, I now smelled of cigarette smoke. Trying to calm down, I opened my book and re-read the last dozen pages I'd tried to read when the old man was there, since I had no idea what I'd just read.

Twenty

Civil Authority Goes Missing and

Doesn't Show Up

Tuesday, August 30, 2005. Late Afternoon

For the most part, I was engrossed in TR's world. As I was reading, I noticed a young couple walking a large, white dog. Oh no,
I thought, more company. However, when they got next to me, the
woman simply smiled and said, "Hello." The man looked over with no
particular expression while they kept moving. Relieved, I went back to
reading, which due to its power to transport me, had taken on great
importance. I started to worry about what I would do if I finished
before I was able to get of New Orleans. To prevent that, I paced my
reading.

Also vying for my attention were the rescue helicopters flying over.
One must have flown over every twenty minutes, but I had no idea
where they were coming from or where they were going. "Why they
weren't stopping to help us?" I wondered. Even though I could ratio-
nalize that they were helping others in greater need, the fact that help
was just that far above my head, but there was no way I could reach it
was maddening. I tried to ignore them.

It was now around 6:30 p.m. and I had been reading most of the afternoon. I looked up and noticed a pink building lit up by that late afternoon sun, glowing gold. Then I saw another pleasant scene of normalcy—three guys sitting and talking on one of those French Quarter wrought-iron balconies. Well, except for the fact that all of the windows and doors on the first floor were boarded over with plywood with big red "X's" painted on them. Normalcy rests on a very shaky foundation, I thought. I desperately wanted to be a part of that scene.

I didn't want to be out on the streets after dark, so I headed back to the hotel. After a full day of heat, the lobby was sweltering and the front desk clerk had no updates. Knowing that we were in for another night, I made my way back up to the ballroom, piled my plate with grits, butter, and white bread, and went in the opposite direction of the software developers. I washed a few bites down with half a glass of tepid water, and went over and asked one of the serving ladies if they had a corkscrew, but she didn't. I thanked her and left.

I made my way to the elevator. I'm somewhat claustrophobic, but normally elevators don't bother me unless they're crowded and someone is in my face. Well, since at most only two out of six elevators were working they were packed. I waited for the elevator with a crowd of people that grew larger by the minute. Finally, the elevator doors opened and disgorged a torrent of humanity. Once they cleared out, there was an immediate rugby scrum, not with as much violence, but with the same competitive spirit, moving towards the doors, and I was right in the middle of it. I wedged myself in near the door with my back against the wall and arms pinned to my sides. The elevator far exceeded the number of people permissible under "normal" societal rules. We had all gone two days without baths, it was stuffy, and we stopped at every floor on our way up. That all added up to the perfect conditions for a claustrophobic hissy fit.

Once the doors closed and we started up, I feverishly scanned the elevator ceiling for the emergency trap-door exit in case I might have to locate it in the dark. I knew for a fact that if that generator failed and we got stuck, I was going to freak out. Checking for that trap door was an indication of how quickly I had shifted over into survival mode, automatically.

Finally, after what seemed like forever, the elevator hit the fifteenth floor, at which point I shot out like a human cannon ball. Sweating profusely, I escaped to my room. I had again been so happy to see the sunlight in the morning that I had opened the drapes and forgotten to close them, and now the room was sweltering so I propped the door open with a chair, hoping to get some air. However, since the hall was almost as hot, the law of thermodynamics wasn't working in my favor.

I had found out that we now had a curfew to be in our rooms by 8 p.m., and it was just past eight now. We all decided to obey that rule, so I guess the hotel still held some sense of order, although diminished, inside its walls. Being a good hotel citizen, I just stuck my head out the door to take a look as I could hear people talking. I could see three women, each sitting separately in the hallway, just at the entrance to their rooms. Feeling like I was pushing the boundaries, I decided to join them and so sat down in my doorway. Besides, whatever transfer of air that was happening, which wasn't much, was going on right there.

I joined in their conversation, and we didn't talk about anything in particular, just what they had heard about rescue, and how they were coping with the heat, the what's-your-story stuff. Finally, aside from my bird buddy from yesterday, here was a bit of companionship and since it was inside the safe walls of the hotel, I welcomed it. It was odd, the four of us sitting in the dimly lit and stuffy hallway, anchoring ourselves firmly to our rooms so as to not break the rules, and talking about the as yet, non-existent rescue. It was straight out of *Waiting for Godot*.

I sat out for maybe half an hour, and then excused myself. The hotel seemed "safe," but I wasn't feeling secure enough to leave my door open for the night, even though it might have provided some movement of air. So here I was, back in my dark room with the only light being my little squeeze light. I sat there on the end of the bed, shining my light around the room until it landed on that bottle of wine, still sitting in pristine unopened condition on top of the dresser. It was starting to drive me buggy.

Finally, I couldn't stand it anymore, so I did something I never do when staying in a hotel; I raided the mini bar refrigerator. It had long since lost any semblance of refrigeration so everything was room temperature. There were three Bud Lights and three Heinekens just sitting there waiting for me. I felt the tops of the bottles and determined that the Buds were the only ones that had twist off tops. I detest Bud, but given the emergency circumstances I very nearly weakened and drank one. Things were getting desperate, but they weren't that desperate.

I grabbed one of the Heinekens and started searching the room to see what I could find that might substitute for a church key (well that's what we used to call them when I was a kid) but found nothing. Frustrated, I walked over and opened the room door and tried to pop the cap in the doorjamb latch, but to no avail. I was going to open that damned bottle.

I came back into the room more frustrated than before. I had a beautiful Heineken in my hand and a great looking bottle of red wine on the dresser, and I couldn't open either one of them. They were doing me as much good as the helicopters that flew overhead all day. I shined my light onto the door looking for anything that might work when I noticed the mechanism that keeps the door from slamming shut, one of those metal gadgets with two arms that come out from the top of the door and meet in a very narrow "V" shape. I thought I'd give it a try. It took two hands to feel for the "V" and then to hold the bottle steady when it was wedged in. That ole dinky light only worked when you were squeezing it, so that was out.

I put the light down, grabbed the Heineken, walked until my fingers touched the back of the door, felt for the closing mechanism, and worked my way to the "V." With one hand grasping the "V" and the other holding the beer, I nestled the rim of the bottle cap firmly into the "V" and gave it a good hard jerk. The bottle, with cap attached, slid out. I gave it three or four more tries, each time having to feel my way back up in the dark until the cap finally popped off. I had jiggled the bottle around so much that when it opened I got a beer shower. I gratefully drank it down.

I raided a second Heineken and repeated the process. I called my wife and found out that the heavy media coverage of the looting was being used as an excuse for not sending in rescue groups. That seemed like a lot of baloney to me. I mean, for God's sake, we were all there and we weren't being killed, so why couldn't the National Guard fight their way in? It made no sense.

I was slipping further into the abyss that was now New Orleans, but I did my best to assure her that it wasn't as bad as it looked on television. We talked for a few more minutes, and I hung up, having no idea what tomorrow would bring.

TWENTY ONE

HINTS OF A RESCUE PLAN

Wednesday, August 31, 2005. Wednesday Morning.

I t was now my fifth day of being trapped by Katrina, and things weren't getting any easier. One way that I coped with the stress, aside from losing myself in TR's life story, was to sleep in. I figured the later I slept since I didn't have any place to go, the less I focused on the heat and chaos. I was putting myself in *suspended animation* or a kind of crisis-induced hibernation. What I wouldn't have given to be in the Arctic Circle just then.

I got up around ten o'clock and went to the window. I could see the floodwater had covered more of the tombs and now was covering everything but the tops of the cars parked outside. I was fairly certain that was about as far as it was going to go from the reports that my wife was giving me, but the sight of that cemetery underwater was chilling.

By now I had run out of clean shirts so I went through my bag and pulled one out of the wad of dirty tee shirts. I grabbed a teacup of water out of the bathtub and brushed my teeth. I'd had it with looking homeless, so I decided to wash my hair. I grabbed the ice bucket and dipped it into the tub. Bending over the sink I spilled just enough to get wet. I grabbed the tiny bottle of shampoo and gave it a whirl around my head, and finished up with a quick rinse. I felt some guilt over using water this way, but my self-esteem was taking enough of a beating from wearing dirty clothes, having no bath, and depending on others for my welfare.

I'm not accustomed to being in such a dependent state. I put myself through college, went on to graduate school, earned a Ph.D., set up and ran my own business, and took care of my family. I was the guy that others depended on, but here I was depending on the hotel to shelter and feed me, and was waiting for the government to free me. I didn't want to ask for any more help.

With dirty clothes, but wet, mostly clean hair, I went down to the lobby and inquired, once again, if they had been able to put their hands on a corkscrew. Of course, they had no corkscrew, and probably thought, "What's with this guy who keeps coming by everyday to ask for a corkscrew?"

I went through the chow line and when I sat down I overheard the people talking at the next table. I wasn't sure that I heard them right so I apologized for eavesdropping and asked what they were talking about. Sure enough, the hotel had privately arranged for ten buses to drive into town and evacuate us and the guests from the nearby Holiday Inn! I could barely contain myself. I asked them where to get tickets.

I raced, I mean raced, down to the lobby where a dozen people were lined up for the front desk. I asked the last person if this was the line for bus tickets and she said that it was. I didn't trust that the news was true, but waited in the barely moving line, terrified that I'd get to the front only to be told that the tickets were sold out.

Finally, I was standing in front of a clerk with a German accent. "Is it true?" Yes, she assured me. "Well, what's the deal," I asked? Ten air-conditioned buses would be in front of the hotel tonight at six o'clock, and they would take us to Houston Hobby Airport, at which point we could individually arrange our way home. The cost per ticket was $45, and we should line up on the street at five o'clock. The only conditions were that if you didn't get a ticket before they sold out you weren't going, if you lost your ticket you weren't going, and finally, if you tried to rush onto the buses when they arrived and cause a ruckus you weren't going. I could live with that so I plunked $45 down in cash and got my prized ticket.

I was leaving this hellish situation in an air-conditioned bus and I was barely able to speak. In another seven hours there would be an end point and that gave me the strength to cope until those buses rolled up.

As I stepped away from the counter I secured my ticket. It was small and red, like one of the old-fashioned movie tickets, which meant I could put it into the deepest recess in my wallet. I pretty much walked around the rest of the day with my hand in my pocket gripping my wallet.

Relieved but fearful that it was too good to be true, I caught the elevator back upstairs in order to grab my camera, book, and some water. Since the local people had been moved out of the hotel, the elevator wasn't nearly as crowded and didn't make so many stops. When I got to my room, I thought about closing the drapes to keep the room from getting so hot, but didn't as I'd be leaving town in just a few hours.

Before leaving the room I called my wife and she was so relieved that she broke down into tears. I told her she could call off the rescue, that I loved her, that I couldn't wait to see her, and that I would call before I left for Houston.

I then phoned Southwest to arrange a flight from Houston for the next morning. I was about to take one final tour around the Quarter and spend the rest of the afternoon in my reading spot. However, as I collected my things I started to worry that maybe we wouldn't get to Houston in time for the early morning flight I'd just booked. What if the buses were late or the traffic was bad or what if a million other things happened to delay us? I rang Southwest again and changed my flight to the afternoon.

Satisfied that I had done all that I could to get myself home and buoyed by the knowledge that the end of my ordeal was within reach, I hit the superheated street for my last few hours in New Orleans.

TWENTY TWO

SOME HOTEL GUESTS GET TO LEAVE

Wednesday, August 30, 2005. Mid-day.

I went out through the garage, and was surprised to see people waiting on the sidewalk, some standing, some sitting on ice chests, suitcases, or on the stoops of the old French doors on the side of the hotel.
I asked what was going on, and the parking attendant told me that
some of the guests and families of hotel employees were able to move
their cars out of the garage.

It turns out that the hotel has a secondary garage just across the
street, in which the majority of the cars are parked. They move cars to
the upper floors by a car elevator, and since the generator power didn't
reach the other building, those parked on the upper floors couldn't
get their cars out. This morning the hotel staff had managed to run a
makeshift electrical cable across the street to power that car elevator.

There was a mixture of people loading up while others waited for
their cars. Right next to the main garage driveway was an older green
Chevrolet, and a middle-aged man in jeans and tee shirt was loading an old woman in a wheel chair into the front passenger seat. Just
behind them was a blue Honda with two guys in shorts and tank tops

loading up, followed by a blue Ford Explorer with a family with two small children. Even though this street was one-way, half the cars were pointed in the wrong direction. With society broken down, there was really no reason to worry about little things like one-way streets.

It was as hot as the day before, if not hotter, and everyone looked worn down. The street was littered with trash, which now smelled of being in the sun too long. Although the release of these cars signaled that things were looking up, envy swelled up in me as I watched them drive away, one by one.

I headed to Bourbon Street and on my way could see that Canal Street was completely flooded. Looking straight ahead on Bienville, I could see the floodwater had come within half a block of Bourbon. I walked to the edge of the water and watched three young men and a woman, all carrying white plastic garbage bags loaded with stuff, splashing through the water. Where were they coming from, I wondered, but more importantly, where were they going? Unless they had friends or relatives with apartments on the high ground, the only place they could go was the Convention Center, a place I'd heard a thousand horror stories about.

I turned away from Canal and headed to reclaim my reading spot. I had read for an hour when I heard a door open, and I saw the young woman and man who had passed me the day before. She was holding the dog leash and he was carrying a very large oven tray that was covered with plastic wrap. When they got near me the woman smiled again and asked if I would like to have some bread pudding. As it turns out, he owned the little bakery cafe at the other end of the pedestrian walkway that I had stopped in on Sunday. Now he looked to be following her lead in the offer of kindness. Since food, and, most importantly water, were constantly in short supply or in the threat of running out, I was always hungry and thirsty so I said, "Yes, I'd love some." If you haven't had bread pudding, if it's done correctly, it will be moist and pudding like on bottom with a nice firm, crunchy top, and that's how this pudding looked.

As I anticipated eating that bread pudding, the guy pulled back the plastic wrap, balanced the large tray on his left hand, and with his right acting as a shovel, scooped up a big hunk of that bread pudding and held it out for me. I offered the palm of my right hand, he plopped it down, and the bread pudding transfer was complete. Under Katrina rules, getting food was the important act, and how I got it didn't matter.

She smiled at me, he looked slightly embarrassed, and I thanked them and took a bite. I assured them that I found it quite delicious and thanked them again. Their, really her, kindness touched me and was one of those fellow-captive moments that I'd been searching for. A minute of pleasantries and they were on their way. I finished the bread pudding and tried to lick the sticky residue off my hand, at least enough so that I could pick up my book.

Another half hour passed in quiet reading when I again heard a door open and looked up to see the old man headed my way. We went through the same routine as the day before. After he left, it was getting on towards four o'clock, so I decided to go back over and get ready to leave. Only two more hours and I'd be in a sweet air-conditioned bus.

I went up to pack and as I did, I grabbed that last Heineken out of the fridge, popped the top in the door mechanism, and enjoyed my last drink in New Orleans.

Sitting on the edge of the bed I stared at that bottle of wine. I wasn't going to take it with me as I had only liberated it for use during my Katrina emergency. I picked it up, walked across the hall, and carefully set it back on the shelf where I found it.

I forgot to mention that when Kaitlin and I stopped at my mother's house in Arkansas on our drive cross-country, I borrowed two old photo albums to scan and make digital copies for my brothers and myself. As a kid, I used to spend hours looking through those albums.

Her photos have never left the house before. I knew if I let anything happen to them I'd have to answer not only to my mother, but also to my three brothers.

As the room was so humid from the rainwater on the drapes and carpet, I worried the pictures might be sticking together. I had taken them out of my bag the day before and checked to make sure they were fine, which they were, and then set them out so that the light from the windows could hit them.

I very carefully put the pictures back together and set them in the middle of my bag so that they were surrounded and cushioned by clothing. I finished packing, looked around to make sure I hadn't forgotten anything, then said goodbye to my room, and to my Katrina experience.

TWENTY THREE

THE AFTERMATH OF LOOTING

Wednesday, August 31, 2005. Late Afternoon.

I asked the desk clerk if I could put my bags behind the counter while I went outside to take a last look around. She said that would be no problem, and reminded me to start lining up at five for the buses. Not to worry, I assured her. There was no way in hell that I was going to miss that bus. It was now 4:30 p.m.

I walked out the main hotel entrance onto Royal and walked over to look at the now looted Walgreens. When I got to the intersection, a man with two large brown paper bags printed "Walgreens" and an additional plastic bag, was crossing Royal. I was surprised that after three days of looting there was anything at all valuable still inside.

A few seconds later another man emerged from Walgreens pushing a shopping cart piled high with stuff, topped off by a grey garbage can. I took a photograph of him from a distance of about thirty feet and wondered if he would "mind" having his picture taken while looting. I quickly put the camera back into its bag, and then looked away. He slowly pushed his cart towards Bourbon. I don't think he cared one way or the other about having his picture made.

The whole scene was a mess. There was trash-filled water in the gutters, and the sidewalk in front of the Walgreens was littered with now soggy paper, discarded boxes, plastic wrappers, and other sour trash.

I entered Walgreens, which resembled nothing of the clean, well-lit store that I had been in on the prior Saturday. The floor was littered with even more trash than was outside, as if a giant had grabbed the building and shook everything off the shelves. There were empty soda cans, candy wrappers, plastic bags, and a variety of small items that apparently weren't worth picking up.

Just inside the door was a Krispy Kreme donut cabinet, and at the end of the next aisle was a Red Bull energy drink refrigerator, both of which had been cleaned out. The shelves behind the front counter, which previously held cigarettes and electronics, were completely empty. The cameras, electronics and film were gone from the shelves behind the photo counter. It was surprising that some shelves still held a good number of items, like hair spray, shampoo, and shaving cream.

I walked over towards the photo counter and found an empty box of "Alligator Bob's Gourmet Alligator Snacks" lying on the floor. A couple of guys were scoping the aisles as another man rode his bike through the store. A man and a woman passed by and he yelled out, "Could I get some help around here? Damn this Walgreens has bad service." His lady friend laughed.

I spied something that intrigued me. I had bought my wife a couple of boxes of Cafe du Monde Beignet mix and I was surprised to see the shelf that held boxes of it hadn't been touched. I thought the looters would go for one of the native New Orleans treats, but, surprisingly, beignet mix wasn't worth looting. I took a couple more pictures and hit the street again.

It was an altogether depressing scene and the fact that the couple thought it was a joke only made it more so. Where am I? What's going on? What's wrong with these people? Those and other questions were running through my head as I walked back to the hotel.

I was determined to get on one of those buses and sit near the front, as the back would be too claustrophobic, especially for eight hours. As I retrieved my bags from the desk clerk, I asked her just exactly where the buses would be, so that I could position myself in what I like to call the "pole position." She wasn't exactly sure, but thought they would be in front on Royal. People were already starting to gather around the front door, so I picked a place in line four people from the front. I put my bags down, sat on the green one, and leaned back against the stone hotel wall.

I was sitting right next to a young thirty-something Canadian woman and her mother. We struck up a conversation as the young woman chain-smoked the time away. They told me that "Dad" hadn't come on this trip and that they couldn't wait to get home out of this mess.

Just about that time, two couples came walking up the street from the other hotel and got in line behind me. They parked their large suitcases almost on top of me and then stood in a semi-circle, blocking any possibility of air circulation, creating a private little "claustrophobic zone" with me now pinned between the stone wall and their legs. I asked one of the ladies if she would mind moving her bag back a bit and she said she that would be fine.

I had escaped the air-pocket trap the four tourists had unwittingly set for me, and I was in no mood for any further invasion of my space when a middle-aged man decided to station himself right next to me instead of going to the end of the line. Once he was in position, he started flirting like mad with the young Canadian woman.

I couldn't believe it. Really, what was this guy thinking? Was he going to invite her up to his room, or was he just a compulsive flirt?

Whatever, it was really getting under my skin. Here we were, stinky as all hell, sweating like pigs, anxious as cats, waiting for our best and only shot at breaking out of our Katrina imposed internal exile and this guy decides it's a good time to try to pick up the Canadian. "Well, more power to you fella," I thought, "but if I weren't such a damned nice guy, I would slug you."

The closer it got to six o'clock the more people came out and lined up along the front of the hotel. We were all, to a person, hopeful that this was our last hour in New Orleans.

TWENTY FOUR

THE BUSES ARE COMING, THE BUSES ARE COMING

Wednesday, August 31, 2005. Early Evening.

The promised hour of six o'clock arrived, with several hundred people lined up on both sides of Royal and around the corner onto Bienville. There were families with small children including infants, old people, couples, singles like me, and small groups. Overflow storm-water filled the gutters to the top of the curb, making the sidewalks narrow and difficult to navigate with all the people and suitcases. An empty shopping cart filled with trash was parked just at the end of the line.

Two New Orleans Police cruisers were parked in the middle of the intersection of Royal and Bienville and five flak-jacketed shotgun-totting officers stood around them. I suppose two hundred-fifty hotel guests with their possessions out on the street in the dark made a pretty tempting target for looters, so I appreciated the hotel management for looking after our security. It was good to see the police finally out of their vehicles, which also indicated the risk was real.

I sweated in line with everyone else, scanning for the buses. Now more guests from the Holiday Inn pulled bags up the street and joined the line including several old people being pushed in wheel chairs. A forklift from the other hotel drove slowly by, deposited a bench for the elderly and went back for another load. We all intently watched this slow motion migration.

About fifteen minutes later, I heard the forklift coming back, and when I looked over, a three hundred-fifty to four hundred pound man was being carried like a load of potatoes on the front. He was sitting sideways, facing us, and his right arm was wrapped around the vertical bar that the lift rides up and down. His feet were bare, his ankles wrapped in what looked like gauze, and his shoes were in his lap. He was talking to the driver, and paid no mind to us. "Way to go, buddy, that you've got the inner strength to do whatever it takes to get yourself out of here," I thought.

We were all exhausted, so our collective reserve of compassion for our fellow man, no matter what their size, was low. I heard one of the women behind me say, "Just look at how fat that man is. I hope he doesn't sit next to me." Her friend wondered aloud if he had had to buy two tickets because of his great size, and how unfair it would be if he only had to buy one.

The forklift operator carefully set him down by the seniors, whereupon several men standing by moved him over to the bench. Once this was accomplished, the driver turned around to collect his next load.

By now it was nearly 7:00 p.m. and Robert, the manager, who seemed to be the one most in charge, stepped into the middle of Royal and asked us to listen up. He had just spoken to the lead bus driver, the buses were on the bridge, and would be here within fifteen minutes. We could just about feel that air-conditioning. He spoke up again to remind us, "If you don't have your ticket or if you rush the buses, you're not going." I knew I wasn't going to do anything that would sink my chances.

For the first time, I could actually start to imagine that this would all be over soon. Mind you, it only lasted a second, and the relaxation did nothing to dial down my revved-up-third-born-competitor who was hell-bent on getting a good seat.

At dusk the buses were nowhere in sight, and the Louisiana mosquitoes appeared. That's when they come out, you know. I must have gotten half a dozen bites in the first few minutes.

The only light came from the fluorescent overhang above the hotel's front doors. Its green and white awning was torn, twisted and hanging down in pieces. Plywood covered one of the front windows. With all the people, trash, and standing floodwater, it looked like an evacuation scene from Bosnia. But where was the evacuation?

The closer we got to 8:00 p.m. the more the collective anticipation grew. I now had time to rethink my best-place-to-stand-to-insure-a-seat-strategy. Maybe I was not in the pole position. What if they came in from the opposite direction and the bus doors were on the other side of the street?

I asked the Canadian gal to watch my bags before I jumped over the floodwater moat and found Robert. I asked him where we "should be" lined up. He said that, yes, the buses were coming from the opposite direction, and would drive up Bienville. I thanked him, turned around, thanked the Canadian for her help, picked up my bags, and found a place around the corner on the curb on Bienville.

I was there no more than five minutes, when people began to queue behind me. A tall gum-chewing teenager planted himself across the street. Every ten-seconds or so he would disrupt the quiet city (no power nor many cars) with a loud pop of his gum. "If I sit next to this kid on a bus for the next eight hours I'll go mental." I knew right then that my patience was now, officially, shot.

As I was strategizing to board a different bus from the *gum popper*, four guys lined up next to me. One of them looked familiar. "You guys getting on the bus?" I asked him as he sat down on the curb.

"Yeah, my name's Brad. I run the bakery cafe around the corner on the walkway."

It was Mr. Bread Pudding. It all fell into place. Not only had he and his girlfriend given me the bread pudding, but he was also the guy that I tried to buy a cup of coffee from on Sunday. He and three of his buddies had decided to head for a relative's house in Arkansas. Brad was then going to catch a flight back to New York, where he was from, and figure out his next move.

"What about your girlfriend?" I asked.

"She decided that she couldn't leave the pets. I told her I couldn't handle it anymore and had to get out of here," he said.

"Man," I thought, "that can't have done much to move the relationship forward." What would I have done in that situation, how do you start that conversation, I wondered.

Brad asked me what I thought would happen to New Orleans. Did I think it would be out of commission long? How soon did I think it would take the tourists to come back? How long before he should return from New York? Did I think he should reopen his shop or just close up and leave New Orleans? Of course, I could only offer banal platitudes which hardly helped Brad feel better.

There must have been something about sitting on that dark curb, waiting for those buses that enabled a conversation like that. Maybe it was more a "right here, right now is all we have" frame. Regardless, I didn't think Brad would be coming back to New Orleans anytime soon.

It was now around 8:15 p.m. and I could hear a commotion from around the corner. Several blocks down, in the opposite direction from where Robert said the buses would be coming, I could see headlights. When we could finally make out that these were, in fact, the buses, a from-the-bottom-of-the-heart cheer went up from the assembled masses.

Wait a minute; there was only one bus. Where were the other nine? What was happening? What the...!?

It, a yellow school bus, pulled up in front of us. There were only about a dozen people on it and Robert boarded to talk to the driver. We gathered around. After an eternity, he stepped off to talk to the police and then went to the driver again. As this was going on, the bus, with the engine still idling, enveloped us in a cloud of diesel exhaust.

Robert walked back over to the police and the other manager. One of the guys near me had overheard part of the conversation and told us that the driver was offering to drive anyone to either the Convention Center or Baton Rouge for a hundred and fifty dollars. I was offended. So were my four buddies. Here we were, stuck and this guy was trying to take advantage! "Why would I pay $150 to go to Baton Rouge without air-conditioning, when I've got a $45 ticket for an air-conditioned super-liner that's going to take me all the way to Houston?" I said. No thank you!

The driver eventually closed the door and slowly drove off into the darkness, leaving us, once again, sitting on that curb. I was growing more restless and more worried.

Nine o'clock came and went as did nine-thirty. Robert had made one announcement that they didn't know exactly what had happened, but they were doing everything they could to get back in touch with the driver. That gave me some confidence. Besides, Robert had a way about him that signaled that he was in charge.

Just past 10 p.m., it was hot, pitch black, mosquito-ridden, and still no buses. I saw a baby asleep on his daddy's shoulder, another child asleep on its mother's lap, and two children lying on a blanket. The police were still standing around the two cruisers with shotguns at the ready adding an element of menace to the scene.

I saw Robert conferencing in the middle of the street with one of the other managers before walking over to the police. I decided to trail Robert and listen in. "The damned buses aren't coming," Robert said to the police. "We have to figure out what to do with all of these people." My heart came completely unhinged and dropped to my feet.

"It seems to me that the only thing we can do is send them over to the convention center," said the other manager. I instantaneously moved from eavesdropper to full-bore active participant.

"Hey, hey, hey! You can put us right back into our rooms, no problem whatsoever," I blurted out. No one in that circle had noticed me until now.

Every head snapped my way, and the large, beefy senior officer said, "Sir, you're going to have to step back. This is a private conversation." His tone meant business, so I turned and walked back over to Brad and the others.

"The buses aren't coming. They have no idea what happened to them," I said.

"No way! Are you kidding me?" Brad asked in disbelief.

"Yeah. They're talking about what to do with us right now. The one manager wants to send us to the convention center." At this point, we were the only ones who knew.

"What are you going to do?" Brad asked me.

"I don't know. I'm going to wait and see what Robert has to say."

Robert, now finished with the conference, walked halfway down the middle of Royal, stopped and shouted, "I need your attention. Everyone, I need your attention." Slowly, word spread down the line that Robert had some news. Everyone got quiet, waiting.

"The buses aren't coming. We have no idea what happened to them. You're all going to have to go back into your rooms. Wait. Wait. We're going to keep trying to find them and we'll make an announcement over the PA system if we do." All hell broke loose.

"What do you mean the buses aren't coming," shouted one.

"We want those buses," called out another.

"We want our $45 back!" said someone else.

"We're not going back in our rooms!" a woman next to me shouted. There was a cacophony of cries, shouts and sobbing.

"Now hold on, hold on!" Robert shouted over the noise. "All right. You don't have to go back into your rooms. You've got a choice. You can go down to the convention center." And with that, the reality of our situation began to weigh on my chest and I found it hard to breathe. And just like that our sure-fire escape had suddenly vanished.

"Now, since we zeroed out all of the door key codes, you're going to have to line up in the lobby and get a new key card for your room." And with that, Robert headed for the lobby.

TWENTY FIVE

BACK INTO THE HOTEL

Wednesday, August 31, 2005. Late Night.

N ow what? Now what? That's all I could think. My mind wasn't able to generate any other thought, nor any answers. The one thought, the one target that I'd been fixated on was the arrival of those air-conditioned buses. I was going to be free of the heat, the humidity, the uncertainty, the deprivation, the strangeness, and the captivity. That all just came crashing down, and every single hope I had lay in little pieces at my feet. I barely had the energy to step over them.

I walked back over to Brad and the guys. "What are you going to do?" Brad asked me.

"It looks like the only choice is to go back into the hotel and hope to God that they find those buses. How about you?" I asked.

"I guess we'll all have to go back home, but how are we going to know if the buses show up?" Brad said.

"If one of you gives me your phone number I'll call you when the announcement comes," I said.

"Really? You would do that?" asked one of the others.

"Sure," I said.

He wrote his name and phone number on the back of one of my business cards that I'd handed him. His name was Mike. With that, they walked off into the dark and I stood there wondering what Brad's homecoming would be like. How do you walk back into your girlfriend's apartment, and face her after walking out and leaving her behind just a few hours earlier? With not much else to feel thankful for at the moment, I thanked God that at least I wasn't in Brad's shoes.

I picked up my bags, which now seemed heavier than when I brought them out, and trudged back down Royal and into the hotel lobby. It was an unbelievable sight; a mass of exhausted, strung-out, sweaty, and extremely frustrated people slumping on the few couches or sitting on the floor. It was difficult to walk without stepping on someone. I maneuvered my way through a narrow path and sat down on the last few steps of the mezzanine stairs. There was a little movement of air between the floors that kept me from feeling too claustrophobic.

A thirty-something woman sat a few steps up from me, crying. Through her tears she said, "Dammit. They should have known better. They should have gotten those buses in here sooner. They should have never let this happen."

I turned and said, "I know. It's awful, but you have to just reach deep down inside yourself and grab another handful of patience. That's all I'm trying to do." That was true too. I was grabbing deep for patience I didn't know I had.

A long line of people waiting to get new room key-cards passed me and stretched to the front door. I decided to wait, so I stayed on the steps turning my face to find any moving air. The woman behind me was still sobbing.

Robert walked into the middle of the lobby and announced that they had finally discovered that the buses had, in fact, been on the bridge at 7:00 p.m. when he spoke with them, but they had been seized by the National Guard, under the authority of martial law, and sent to the Superdome. Further, "We're going to keep trying to find more buses and if we do we will make an announcement over the P.A. system for all of you to come down. It doesn't matter if it's 2 a.m., or 4 a.m., or whatever time, we'll keep trying, so be ready to go at a moment's notice." What? I couldn't believe it. OUR buses had been seized that we had paid for? That wasn't fair, but fair was a concept from the my pre-Katrina life, and it just didn't matter here.

Once the commotion began to die down, Robert announced that the hotel had just a couple of cases of bottled water left, which they were going to distribute. We were to go see a designated hotel worker to get our one bottle of water. He was just to my right, so I jumped up, took the few steps towards him, and got my bottle. I sat back down and tried to sniff out the moving air.

The best word that I can think of to describe the scene in there is this: wilted. Everyone, everything was just wilted. There were no more straight lines including people. When people stood up they slumped. When they sat down they leaned. I was wilted too.

After half an hour the line was more manageable so I joined in. How many lines had I been in over the last several days? How many days had I been here? I couldn't remember. This was my new normal. It was the world of "Mad Max," the "Road Warrior" come true and it was now my world.

After getting a new key card, I got back up to my room. I found a chair and propped the door open. I was more worried about suffocating than I was about someone coming in the room while I was asleep. Opening the door didn't circulate any air, but having it open did make me feel less boxed in. I called Kathy, who by now was frantic to hear from me. Since my cell phone didn't work and I had been out on the street, it had been over seven hours since we'd spoken.

She couldn't believe the story I told her. She had called the "800" number for the hotel and had been told that we had left hours ago for Houston on the buses. It was easy to see how they got that wrong in that the call center was located in Canada. I assured her that, indeed, I was back in my room. She broke down in tears.

She told me that my brother Brian had somehow networked his way to our late stepfather's niece, Carol, who lived in Baton Rouge, which is where I needed to go. It was only a little over an hour drive north of New Orleans, but it might as well have been on the other side of the country as far as my ability to reach it.

My brother, Mike, who lives in California, told me the night before that he wished he was there with me. My other brother, Steve, was doing what he could. My son goes to school with George Lucas's son and Kathy even called his assistant, Sushma, to see if George could do anything to help. She said she'd see what she could do.

My nephew, Blake, who lived in Arkansas, told Kathy that he'd been thinking of different plans that sounded kind of crazy, but that might work. He was thinking that he and a couple of friends would drive their truck as close to New Orleans as possible. They would then drive dirt bikes on back roads into the city, find me, and spirit me out of town. He also thought maybe they could launch a boat and come down the river, land at New Orleans, find me and motor back up to where they left the truck. Either way, they were prepared, he told her, to shoot their way in and out if necessary. God bless all of them.

Before hanging up, Kathy said, "You're such a sound sleeper, I'm just afraid that if they do make an announcement, you'll sleep right through it."

"Don't be silly," I assured her. "The P.A. system is really loud and there is a speaker in each room. If they find more buses there's no way I'm missing any announcement."

By now, my facade of "I'm fine," had broken down. I told Kathy, "Honey, you've got to find a way to get me out of here." It was the first time that I had let her know the depth of my longing to come home. "I don't want to be here anymore." She said that she knew and that she was working as hard as she could to make that happen. After realizing that I had likely scared her to death, I half-heartedly told her that, really, I was fine. I told her I loved her, she did the same, and we hung up.

I went over to the mini-bar fridge, opened it and did something I never thought I'd do; I grabbed a Bud Light, twisted off the cap, and drank it. I called Brian to see if he could drive down and find a way he could get through to New Orleans. He said that he'd thought about that, but had been warned by the State Police that he knew in Arkansas not to try that, as there were roadblocks on every road into New Orleans. I said, "Look Brian, I'm out of Heinekens, I just drank a Bud Light, and you know that means that I'm desperate." We both got a laugh out of the absurdity of that. I told him I'd call him tomorrow to let him know where we were with the buses.

It was now well past midnight. I moved over to sleep in the other double bed by the windows. I thought if there was any transfer of air from the room to the hall it might be there. I tried again to open the windows, but one hundred twenty-nine years of paint held firm. The white sheets stuck to me when I turned over.

I thought about taking a chair and breaking out one of the windows. No one would have blamed me for such a desperate act, but I decided against it. Not only could glass falling from fifteen stories really hurt someone, I was far to "well behaved" to do it. One more night in that room, I thought, and that window would have to go.

Sweating like a pig, worrying about missing the P.A. call for the buses, exhausted from living in "Mogadishu" in America, and not feeling one scintilla of air movement, I slowly fell into another fitful night of sleep.

TWENTY SIX

WAKING UP, ABANDONED

Thursday, September 1, 2005. Morning.

I t was near impossible to get any decent sleep. I woke up and glanced at my wristwatch. It was 8 a.m. (I never change my watch when I travel so the local time was actually 10 a.m.) Since my door was open, I could hear voices out in the hallway. Through the fog of waking up, it began to dawn on me that I hadn't heard any announcements about buses being located. Disappointed, exhausted and with no place to go, I dozed back off.

After getting a bit more sleep, I woke up, looked at my watch, and it was now 9 a.m. (11 a.m. local time). I could still hear people talking in the hall. "God, I'm still here," I thought. "I'm never going to leave." I drifted back off.

Forty-five minutes later and I woke up again. It was quiet. I froze and listened, but I couldn't hear anyone talking out in the hall. I got up, walked over to the door, stuck my head out into the hall, and didn't see anyone. "That's odd," I thought.

GREGORY A. KETCHUM PH.D.

I came back inside, picked up the phone and dialed the front desk to see what was happening. The phone still worked and it rang twenty-five to thirty times: no answer. "That's weird," I thought. "Maybe I dialed the wrong number."

I hung up and dialed "O" for the hotel operator. Again, twenty-five to thirty rings later, there was no answer. "That is weird," I thought. "Maybe I dialed wrong a second time." I thought about that for a second. "How could I dial wrong? All I did was push 'O.' How the hell could I get that wrong?" I was trying to find a rational explanation as my heart beat faster.

I threw on my tee shirt, shorts and sandals and headed for the one elevator that still worked. Since this one didn't come to my floor, and was in a different part of the building, I had to go down my hallway, take the emergency stairs one flight to the fourteenth floor, and then reverse directions and cut back across the hotel to the elevator.

As I ran across the fourteenth floor I passed many rooms that had the doors propped open. Each one after the next was empty. I saw several trays with dirty plates on them, sitting on the floor just outside the room. Some even had leftover food. They looked like they had come from breakfast this morning. My heart and feet sped up.

I finally got to the elevator, relieved to see that it still was in operation. I pressed the call button and waited.

Damn! Where is the elevator? Finally, the doors creaked open and I hopped in. I hit the button for the first floor. My mind and heart were racing far faster than that old elevator could go. Finally, I got to the first floor, the doors opened, I popped out, rounded the corner, and was met by my worst fear; the lobby was completely empty. I had been abandoned.

"No, that's not possible," I thought, despite facing the evidence right there in front of me. The lights were on, papers were on the front counter, and everything was the same as the night before, except all of the people were gone.

I yelled out, "Is anyone here? Is anyone here?" No answer. I ran across the lobby. I looked over and the front doors were chained and padlocked shut.

My God, my one chance to get out of this hellhole and I missed it! At that moment, my greatest fear was the thought of facing my wife and telling her that she was right, I slept through the P.A. announcements. "Get on with it man. Find the damned people!" I began to move again.

I ran up the mezzanine stairs and down the hall to the hotel executive offices yelling, "Is anyone here?" as I ran from locked door to locked door. Silence.

I ran back downstairs. I didn't know if I could even get out of the hotel, let alone find the people. I ran out to the garage exit, my heart pounding so loud that I could feel it in my ears. The sliding glass door was jammed open, leaving about a twelve-inch gap. I tried to push it further open, but it wouldn't budge. I was able to wedge myself through.

I now knew I could get out, but I didn't know where everyone went, and most importantly, what I was going to do. I decided to try to find them. Maybe I could spot the buses on the street, or maybe the buses were at the Holiday Inn loading up right now.

I ran through the lobby, caught the elevator up to fourteen, ran across the hotel and up to my room, threw my things together and flew back downstairs.

As I was running across the lobby in the direction of the garage, I was startled to see, through the glass front doors, two New Orleans Police SUV's and four officers in bulletproof vests, with guns drawn. The SUV's were parked in the middle of Royal, two officers were in the street, and the other two were up on the sidewalk right in front of the hotel doors.

One of the officers saw me and yelled out, "There's someone in there." "Thank God. I'm saved," I thought. The officer tried the door.

"You'll have to go around to the garage," I shouted. She understood me, so they got in their vehicles and backed down Royal. Feeling elated, I ran out to the garage.

As I rounded the last corner, I could see that they had backed both vehicles all the way into the garage, in a defensive posture. I squeezed myself and my bags through the small opening and two of the officers walked towards me, guns still in hand. "Where are all the people? What happened to the people?" I asked, in desperation.

"We have no idea. We heard that one of our officers was down here, so that's why we came," said the one closest to me.

By now, I was standing right next to an SUV. "What do you mean you don't know? I pleaded.

"Sir, we have no idea in the world where the people are. We just came to retrieve our officer," he said.

"Well, I haven't seen any officer," I replied.

I still didn't know if I slept through the announcement or what happened to the people. In addition to figuring out what I should do next, I was stuck on solving that mystery. I just couldn't believe that they had left me behind. "Well, just what do you suggest that I do?" I asked him.

"About the only thing you can do is go to the Convention Center," he said blandly.

"You're kidding, right?" I asked.

"No sir, that's about all you can do right now."

"Well, can you guys at least give me a ride down there?" I asked.

"No, we can't really do that. If we drive down there in these police vehicles, we're going to draw gun fire," he said.

"You're joking, right?" I stammered.

"No sir, I'm not," he said.

Wait a minute. These folks were heavily armed, in fast vehicles, and they wouldn't drive me to the Convention Center, but they were suggesting that I just walk over there by myself. I was struggling to comprehend what he was saying and what that meant when he said, "Good luck." With that, they got back in their vehicles and sped off.

So there I stood, in the hot deserted garage, with one bag over my shoulder and one in my hand.

I realized now, in a way that I hadn't before, that this wasn't just an uncomfortable situation, but rather was a downright dangerous one; I could lose my life.

I had waited for the federal, state or local governments to help us. I had waited for the Red Cross, the National Guard, the Salvation

Army and any other aid organization to help us. I had depended on the hotel management to take care of us. They had all, finally, failed.

As I stood there by myself, my thoughts became clear; if I was going to ever get out of New Orleans alive, it was going to be because of my own efforts. I had to find my own way out. I had to make a fundamental switch from looking outside for authority figures to make the decisions and make it happen for me to looking inside of myself. I had to trust my own instincts to lead me out. I walked out of that garage. I knew I wasn't coming back.

Twenty Seven

Finding My Own Way Out of New Orleans

Thursday, September 1, 2005. Mid-day.

M y first goal was to find the missing people and, hopefully, then the buses too. My best shot was the Holiday Inn, and as I briskly moved towards it, the sole of my left sandal peeled back several inches and began to flop. Normally, that would be no big deal, but today, I needed shoes.

When I got to the Holiday Inn corner, a half-dozen young mothers were standing and tending to their kids. I asked them if there was anyone at the hotel. The answer was "no." I realized then that I had no option but to go check out the convention center.

When I asked for directions, one of the women said, "We're going down there sir if you'd like to walk with us." Her kindness stood in marked contrast to the chaos.

"That would be great," I said.

I stood there a few minutes, and the longer I stood and thought about the morning, the greater my urgency was to move on. Walking with this group would only slow me down. Despite their kindness, I told them I was going to go on.

I walked a couple of blocks and then cut over to Canal St., where I came upon two guys loading their car. Awkwardly, I approached them. "Are you guys leaving town?" I asked.

"Yeah, we are," one said as he put another bag in the car.

"Well, I need a ride. Do you guys have room for one more? I asked apprehensively.

"I don't really think so. We've got a lot more stuff to pack and there's barely room for the two of us," he said without looking at me.

"Okay, can you tell me how to get to the convention center?" I asked.

"Well, you go up Canal Street to the Casino and turn right, but if I were you I wouldn't go down there," he replied.

"Why not?" I asked.

"There's some bad shit going on down there." I turned and headed up Canal.

I felt driven to see if the convention center held anything for me. The further I walked the heavier my bags felt, and the stronger an *urge* grew in my heart to throw things away to lighten my load. It was a very primal feeling, one of those survival impulses that kick in automatically. If you've never experienced that it's a surprising and scary feeling. I stopped to see if there was anything I could throw out. After rummaging through my clothes and catching my breath, I decided that it wasn't quite yet time to throw things overboard.

I zipped my bag and started walking when I looked over and noticed a large ABC News satellite truck parked on the streetcar tracks in the middle of Canal. I hustled over to it. "Do you know where the CBS crews are?" I asked, now out of breath.

"I haven't seen them, but they might be down towards Bourbon," he said. I began walking down the line of news trucks that stretched for several blocks. When I encountered trucks that weren't marked, I would stop and ask if they were CBS: no luck.

As I approached Bourbon, I came upon a group of CBS vehicles with four guys talking in front of them. I introduced myself. "My name is Dr. Greg Ketchum. I'm the CBS 5 Workplace and Career Expert for the San Francisco CBS affiliate. I've been stuck in New Orleans for a week now and need a ride out. Are you guys leaving today?"

"Yeah, we're leaving in about half an hour because it's too dangerous to be down here," said one of them.

"Could you take me with you?" I asked.

A young guy, who looked to be "on-camera talent" said, "Well, we really don't have that much room. I'm even going to have to ride in the satellite truck myself. We might have room in there, but I really don't know for sure." My stomach tightened.

What seemed like minutes passed before a guy behind me said, "I've got room in my van. You can ride with me, but we're only going to Kenner, which is about ten miles away."

"Hey, I don't care where you're going. I've got to get out of here," I told him. If he had told me I was to ride on the luggage rack of his van, I swear to you I'd have done it.

I set my bags down. Jim Krasula, a national correspondent for CBS Radio Network, based in Charlotte, N.C., was the one who offered me the ride. As I stood there letting the relief start to sink in, I wondered, could I really trust this? What could I do to boost the chance that they'd actually take me?

I decided to pursue a strategy to make them connect with me as an individual, instead of seeing me as just some guy off the street; I would become a "super-networker." I went up to each person and introduced myself, showed them pictures of my children, and asked about their families and where they were from. The more I met, the more secure I began to feel.

After making the rounds of introductions, I saw an unfamiliar guy walk up to the group and announce, "We just got a call from Bob, a V.P. at a CBS affiliate station. He says he has three elderly relatives stuck at the convention center, and he wants us to get them and drive them out of New Orleans." If they did that, guess who was low man on that totem pole?

While Jim was packing his van, the group began to debate whether they could meet his request. "It's pretty dangerous to go down there," said one.

"How in the world would we know who they are and be able to find them in that crowd?" asked another.

The young "on camera talent" spoke up. "Are we sure that these are Bob's relatives and not just some friends of his? That would be just like him to try to get us to go down there with a bullshit story about his old relatives," he said. If I was going to get tossed out it would be this guy, I decided.

While they were having this discussion I quickly hatched another plan. Figuring it would be harder for them to throw me out of the car than it would be to prevent me from getting in, I picked up my bags and quietly set them inside the back of Jim's van. To my relief, no one noticed.

I walked back over to hear the end of the discussion about the relatives. Led by the young guy, they had come to a consensus; if the old folks could make their own way from the convention center to us in the next fifteen minutes, they could come along. I knew that meant I was probably safe. Even if they could somehow get word to them to come on down, the walk itself was longer than that. It was a faux solution.

I felt bad for the folks, but realistically, there was just no way. If they drove down to the convention center, people wanting food, water or a ride would mob them. Besides, it *was* too dangerous.

The New Orleans Police were out on the street guarding the news crews. From time to time a truck from Wildlife and Fisheries would drive by pulling a boat loaded with a half-dozen fully armed, flak-jacket-helmet-and-goggle-wearing-military-style-police-officers. They looked edgy and ridiculous, but I knew they meant business.

We were about ten minutes from leaving when I looked up Canal Street toward the convention center and saw the four people from the Holiday Inn who had been next to me in the bus line. Actually, they were the very people who had surrounded me with their suitcases and blocked off my air yesterday. I now realized there had been no buses. I felt immediate relief.

I ran to meet them and they recognized me. "What the hell happened this morning?" I asked.

"Well, the hotel told us they were out of food and water and that there was no place else for us to go but the convention center. They gave us maps and sent us on our way," one of the men said.

121

"Where are you going then?" I asked, as they were walking away from the center.

"We walked down and took a look and there's no way in hell we're going to stay there." Next came the question that I hoped they wouldn't ask; "What are you going to do?"

What am I going to do? What am I going to do? It was two questions; what was I going to tell them I was going to do, versus what I was actually going to do?

I don't know how long I paused. If I told them I had a ride I knew that they'd beg me to take them too. That's what I would have done. If I told the CBS guys that I now had four friends with their luggage who wanted a ride as well, I was afraid they would call the whole thing off. They could have rightly said they didn't have the room, and it wouldn't be fair just to take one person. Besides, there realistically wasn't room for them anyway. I hesitated, mulling over this moral dilemma.

"I'm just going to hang out with these guys for awhile," I finally said. "What are y'all going to do?"

"We have no place to go," one of the women said.

"Well, the back door of the hotel is jammed part-way open and you can get in there. That's your best shot," I said, trying to help them in a way that I could.

"Good luck," they said.

"Good luck to you as well," I said. And with that, they walked off towards the hotel.

I couldn't believe what I had just done, but I knew it was the only way. I made a decision to boost the odds of my own survival when I might have been able to provide more help to someone else. I mean, I didn't even know them. Under normal life circumstances it would have been an easy call to bring them along, but making a decision like that while in full-on survival mode is a different story all together. Unless you've been there you have no way of knowing what you'd do. Still, it was one of those moral decisions that I would revisit, over and over again.

Finally, it was time to leave. I started to get into the back of the van and ride in the cargo space, when Jim motioned for me to come and sit in the seat behind him. I moved up, but didn't want to make any move that might have him change his mind. Whether I got out of New Orleans today was, at this moment, totally up to Jim. I felt like a child.

Traveling with Jim was Cami McCormick, another CBS Radio correspondent, who was sitting in the front passenger seat. Just before starting the van, Jim offered me a beer and some trail mix. "Thank you all-powerful father," I thought.

The caravan of five CBS vehicles, with a New Orleans Police cruiser at either end, pulled out for Kenner. I had no idea where that was, nor how far away, but it was out of New Orleans.

Our route took us down towards the convention center, but we turned by the Doubletree Hotel, a couple blocks before it. As we made that turn I spied the first National Guard troops in full battle gear, M-16's at the ready. Their steel cold expressions combined with the positions they had taken around the hotel, told me they were protecting themselves, not us.

It started to rain. We passed many people including an old man, in terrible shape, pushing an old woman in a wheelchair through the rain toward the convention center. Our caravan drove on.

We drove up the on-ramps to the bridge that crosses the Mississippi leading to the "West Bank." Hundreds of people found shelter from the rain under the overpass amidst tons of trash. Others were going up the on-ramps, hoping to walk across the bridge. We passed a small pick-up with perhaps fifteen people standing up in the bed, whipped around by the wind and rain. One man was shirtless.

At mid-span, I was now officially out of New Orleans. I was headed for Kenner, not knowing if I had just jumped out of the frying pan into the fire. I didn't care.

Twenty Eight

Partway to Freedom

Thursday, September 1, 2005. Early Afternoon.

We traveled on back streets, driving around downed trees and power lines. Thirty minutes later we arrived in Kenner, the temporary "base camp" for the CBS News crews. Several large satellite trucks were parked in front of a building, from which most of its bricks had blown down and smashed into two parked cars. The rest littered the parking lot.

A Blackhawk helicopter landed in a field just behind us. "Will you have the sound of that chopper in one of your stories?" I asked Jim.

"Hey, the sound of choppers in the background always makes it a great story," Jim said, smiling.

We were parked next to a Radisson Hotel with several shattered windows. Was it open? When I walked into the lobby the hotel manager immediately approached me in what felt like a very confrontational manner. "Can I help you sir?" he asked.

"Yes, are you open?" I asked.

"No sir, our last guests are leaving right now," he replied.

"I need to get to Baton Rouge. Do you know of anyone going that way? I asked.

"No sir, I'm afraid not. The best you can do is ask someone with a car for a ride," he replied. "I'm sorry I can't be more help and for being so forward in confronting you in the lobby. You just can't be too careful right now."

I approached people loading their car in front of the entry. No, they didn't have any room for an additional passenger. I crossed the street and walked by the two brick-smashed cars, looking inside for keys. Had I found keys and been able to start one of them, I was going to take it and drive myself to Baton Rouge, cracked windshield, smashed hood and all. I didn't know what I would do with the car once I got there, but that detail wasn't important at the moment. Neither car had keys.

I walked up the line of parked CBS vehicles and noticed John Roberts, who at that time was anchoring the CBS Evening News. He was dressed in neatly pressed khaki trousers, a "safari" shirt, and his hair was nicely done. I took one look at him and thought, "Well John, it's clear that you haven't spent anytime in New Orleans yet."

I went back over and borrowed Jim's phone to call my wife. She told me that if I could get to Baton Rouge, my late stepfather's niece, Carol, would take me to their house, where Brian would pick me up the next morning. I thought that was a great plan as well, but I hadn't found a way to get there. Carol had tried to drive to Kenner to get me, but had been turned back at a roadblock just outside of Baton Rouge.

Kathy also told me that one of Brian's friends had a private plane and was ready to fly down to pick me up if I could only get to the

New Orleans airport. "The weather is so bad I wouldn't get on a small plane, plus I have no idea where the New Orleans airport is," I told her. Little did I know then that the airport is actually in Kenner.

When we had driven in I had noticed a Louisiana Highway Patrol station on the other side of the freeway. I screwed up my courage and asked Jim if he could drive me over to see if I could find a way to Baton Rouge through them. "No problem," he said.

Jim pulled into the parking lot, which was crowded with highway patrol cars and vehicles from other police departments. While Jim waited in the car, I walked in and explained my situation to the officer at the front desk. "Do you know of anyone or have any officers who might be going to Baton Rouge?" I asked.

"No sir, we can't spare any officers to drive you up there," he replied. I didn't bother to explain that I was simply hoping to ride with someone.

"Well, do you have any other suggestions as to how I might get there?" I asked.

"The freeway on-ramp that takes you north to Baton Rouge is just over there. You might try hitchhiking," he said. I walked back out and got in the van with Jim.

"Any luck?" he asked.

"No. No luck."

We drove back over to the Radisson and I decided to take a look at how many cars were taking the freeway north. I stood on the corner watching for fifteen minutes and no more than half a dozen cars took the on-ramp toward Baton Rouge. It didn't seem wise to give up the seat in Jim's van to try hitchhiking.

As I walked back, a couple pulled into the closed Shell service station next to us to use the pay phone. I waited for the man to hang up and asked if they were going to Baton Rouge. He politely told me that they might be the next day. I thanked him and returned to the van.

When I got back, Jim had just finished broadcasting a report. He asked me if I'd mind giving an "eyewitness" account for CBS Radio and within a couple of minutes I was on air relaying my story. As I finished, the gentleman from the gas station motioned for me to come over by his car.

I walked back over and he pointed to two young men, who were standing by the pay phone, and said, "These two gentleman might be able to help you." I thanked him, at which point he got in the car and drove off. His kindness touched me.

I introduced myself to two guys wearing "CBS News" caps, and asked if they were going to Baton Rouge. "Well, we usually do each night, but we won't know if we're going tonight for about an hour. That's when they will tell us if we are done for the day," one of them said.

"Well, if you do go, can I ride with you?" I asked.

"Sure," he said.

Their names were Michael and Bill, they were both from New Orleans, and had been hired by CBS News to be local guides. They would drive to Baton Rouge each night, buy water, food, and gasoline, and then bring it back the next morning. They were pulling an aluminum fishing boat that they used to ferry the news crews around in the floodwaters.

Before they left to go see if they were done for the day, I made them promise to come and find me. I told Jim that I might have a way out, but he said that I could stay with him in the van as long as I needed. I began to settle down.

About an hour later, I found Michael and Bill who had just been released and were, in fact, driving to Baton Rouge. I ran back to Jim's van to get my things, my heart racing.

It was hard to leave Jim. In the short time that we had been together, he had become my "guardian angel." When I said goodbye, he said that he didn't really do much, but that he was glad that he could at least help out one person in this whole mess. I swore I'd never forget him.

Michael's truck was a "king-cab" and I expected to sit in the tiny back seat, but Bill insisted that I sit in front. "Is that gas I smell?" I asked.

"Yeah," Michael said, "on the drive down yesterday we spilled a gallon in the cab. I know it's pretty bad." I felt like I had my nose jammed into the end of a gasoline pump hose. Never mind that the smell had me feeling like I might throw up or that we might blow up from even a small spark, I was headed north.

The drive north took just over an hour. "So what's your story?" I asked them at one point. I meant, what do you do, how do you like working with CBS, and stuff like that.

Turns out that Michael was actually a minister for a small Pentecostal church and waited tables on the side to make ends meet. Bill was heavily involved in the church as well.

This might explain how they interpreted my question about "their story," as "How did you first come to know the Lord?" They didn't try to convert me and their testimonies took my mind off the fumes. Bill told me about the time he spent at a small Christian college back East. In fact, he had been recruited to play football. "Oh, how did that happen?" I asked.

"Well, the head of the college at first thought they'd have an 'all preachers' football team, but that didn't work out too well. They kept losing, so they decided they had to change that rule and that's when I got recruited," he said.

"Imagine that, an all preachers football team," I thought. We drove on.

When we rolled into Baton Rouge the city lights were on. All the stores were open, the shopping centers were busy, and the traffic lights worked. It was a shocking re-entry, so close to New Orleans, but like another world.

I offered to buy the boys dinner and they said it wasn't necessary, but that it would be fine. We stopped at a Texas barbecue chain restaurant. While the cool air in Jim's van and Michael's truck was nice, it was nothing like walking into that restaurant. "I'll never take air-conditioning for granted again," I thought.

The restaurant was full of people sitting back, eating, talking, laughing and smoking. Table after table was loaded down with massive plates of barbecue, beer, wine, Cokes and ice water.

As we walked past all those tables I thought, "They have all the water they want and they're not even drinking it." I felt like collecting the full glasses of ice water to bring to our table.

I studied the pictures on the enormous menu and finally settled on a small barbecue plate. After my Katrina rations, those "Texas sized" portions were just too much.

What was familiar was now completely alien. I wanted to stand up and shout, "Don't you people know what's going on in New Orleans? Don't you give a damn?"

When our food arrived I could only pick at mine. Something didn't feel right about taking that much for myself. Michael and Bill had great appetites and I was amazed to watch the ease with which they ate. I called Carol to tell her where to pick me up and then said goodbye to the boys.

TWENTY NINE

MY LONG TRIP FINALLY COMES TO AN END

Thursday, September 1, 2005. Evening.

It only took Carol and her husband, Joe, twenty minutes to drive from their house to the restaurant. I had never met them before, and prior to Katrina didn't even know they existed. Yet, here I was riding in the backseat of their air-conditioned car on the way to spend the night at their house. But, given the events of the last week, nothing surprised me.

They graciously opened their home to me, which stood in stark contrast to the "every man for himself world" I'd come from. I felt as if I had just stepped out of the Nineteenth into the Twenty-first Century. Everything was a novelty: electricity, hot and cold running water, air-conditioning, television, refrigeration, even food.

I was filthy so I took my first shower in five days. I lingered, letting the water run over my face and rest of my body, but felt guilty for taking so much for myself. I stepped out and grabbed a clean, white towel. I flushed the toilet just to watch it work.

Back in my room, I put on a dirty shirt and pair of shorts while Carol washed some of my other clothes. Now that I was clean I got the full impact of my unwashed clothes. I went to the window air-conditioner and put my face where I could feel the full flow of cool air, which brought such relief, but more guilt. Why was I the recipient of all these wonderful gifts?

Carol knocked and delivered a load of freshly laundered clothes. Selecting a Hotel Monteleone tee shirt and khaki shorts, I dressed and began to feel a little like myself. At the same time though, I felt like a tuning fork, set in motion by Katrina, and I was still vibrating.

I called Kathy to let her know I was safely at Carol's and then Brian to coordinate my morning pick-up. He would drive down with a farmer friend, Herman, and meet me around 10:00 a.m.

In the kitchen, Carol offered me food and drink. I wasn't hungry, but I happily accepted a tall, gorgeous, and very cold beer.

I watched a little television with them. An angry New Orleans Police Lieutenant was telling his story to a news anchor on one of the Baton Rouge stations. He had driven his family in his police cruiser from New Orleans to Baton Rouge and dropped them off at a relative's house. He then drove his cruiser to a shopping mall and abandoned it in the parking lot.

"Why did you do that?" asked the anchor.

"We were overwhelmed and the leadership of the city of New Orleans failed miserably. There was no plan to handle a crisis like this, even though this is exactly what we feared could happen," he said.

"What do you mean there was no plan? You mean the plan was outdated?" the anchor asked.

"No. It's not that the plan was outdated, there WAS NO PLAN," he added. "We had no emergency plan. We were told to show up for our normal shifts and do the best we could," he said bitterly. "What the...!?!?" I thought.

Feeling wiped out, I excused myself and went to my room. Being able to close the door and not suffocate or worry about someone breaking into my room was such a luxury. Before dropping off to sleep I turned up the window air-conditioner and made some notes in my journal. My mind was racing, trying to make sense of the last week. Finally exhausted, I switched off the light, slid between the fresh sheets and fell instantly to sleep.

The next morning, I awoke around 9 a.m. and had a light breakfast with Carol and Joe. By 9:30 a.m. I was anxiously listening for the sounds of a truck driving up to the house. At 10:00 a.m. Brian and Herman pulled into the drive. I ran out and gave him a big hug and kiss on the cheek. He's my baby brother, but here he was rescuing me.

I thanked Carol and Joe, invited them to come and stay with us in California, and threw my bags in the back of the king cab. Since Brian and Herman didn't know what to expect, they had planned for total self-sufficiency. An ice chest packed with drinks and sandwiches was in the back of the truck along with a fifty-gallon drum of diesel fuel. A pump and hose was attached to the drum, as was a car battery to power it so that they didn't have to depend on finding open gas stations. Not knowing how dangerous it might be, they both had pistols with them. "Thank God for these Arkansas boys," I thought.

The drive to Arkansas took us around seven hours. Along the way we passed long lines of utility repair trucks heading south. The boys were keenly interested in hearing my story so I told them, and doing so helped me stay grounded and begin my transition back.

I marveled at being back in a world that worked. Speeding along in that truck was a novelty as was seeing all of the other moving vehicles and people going about their normal lives.

We arrived back at my mother's house, a place that I hadn't expected to see again this soon. I was thrilled to be back in her home, and seeing me in the flesh took about a thousand pound weight off her shoulders. After hugs and dinner, we settled down in the living room and I told my story again. In addition to my mother, Brian's wife Rita was there as were my brother Steve and his wife Sally. When I told them about not being able to light that little oil lamp I had taken from the Carousel Bar, I broke down sobbing. Steve moved over to sit next to me and put his arm around me. Normally, I see myself as the strong one, but here I was, spent and being propped up by my brothers. It felt good.

The next morning, Saturday, Steve and Sally drove me to Little Rock to catch my flight home. I had finally managed to reschedule my Southwest flight to a day and place where it would actually happen. On the drive over, we stopped at a gas station and went inside the mini-mart. As Steve was paying for the gas we could see the Katrina headlines of the newspaper on the counter. "You know," Steve said to the cashier, "my brother just came from there" as he pointed to the headline.

"Is that right?" she asked. "Well, God bless you Honey."

As a final stop we went to the Cracker Barrel, which is a chain of "country style" restaurants in the South. The food was wholesome and the portions were huge. I again picked at my food while Steve and Sally enjoyed a full breakfast. I was amazed at all of the food and water, and had that feeling of almost being sick at the sight of it.

On my way out of the hotel I had carried a little green bag with three small half-filled bottles of water. As I got back into Steve's car, there it sat on the floor right in front of my seat. Not having enough food was one thing, but not enough water was something else altogether. I have that bag and bottles out in my car. I still can't let them go.

After Steve and Sally dropped me off, I made my way to my gate. As I sat waiting I made notes in my journal. Everything in the terminal worked. The people were normal, moving through experiences that they expected to happen: waiting for a flight, boarding, and getting to their destination. Having just come from days where few, if any, of my expectations of "normalcy" were met, I was feeling ill at ease. I wanted to get up and scream, "I've just come out of New Orleans. It's a nightmarish hellhole. Wake up people, we've got to do something."

We boarded and I managed to get an aisle seat at the front of the plane next to a nice tall young man named Congo and his mother. We had a pleasant conversation prior to takeoff and then again on our flight to Las Vegas, where we had a half-hour stopover, before proceeding on to Oakland. I didn't believe that I would actually make it home.

About halfway to Vegas we hit turbulence and I began to feel airsick, which rarely happens to me. With only twenty minutes to go before landing I began to feel really sick. The seat belt sign was on so I felt I couldn't leave my seat. I didn't want to throw up in the bag, so I fixed my gaze on the red heart logo on the front wall of the craft. I was feeling more and more anxious.

The flight attendants seated in front of me could see that I was turning white so one got up and handed me a wet cloth and advised me to turn the air vent directly on my face. These helped only slightly so they gave me the okay to hit the bathroom, even though the plane was bouncing hard.

I barely got in the door before I threw up multiple times into the sink. I sat down on the closed toilet seat and tried to get my bearings. All of this had brought on a kind of claustrophobic panic, a feeling that I couldn't stand another minute on that plane.

Once I felt as stable as I was going to get, I went back to my seat and tried to breathe deep and stay focused on that heart logo in front of me. Another five minutes of hanging on and we were on the ground. Once the Vegas passengers had deplaned, I asked the flight attendant if it would be okay if I stood in the walkway just outside the plane. "That would be fine," she said.

As I inhaled fresh air, I debated whether to get back on or not. I really didn't think I could handle a second flight, but I so badly wanted to get home.

When everyone had boarded, I finally forced myself back onto the plane. We had a new flight crew, but they could tell that I was in bad shape. As soon as we left the ground I could feel the nausea and panic swell up, and they could see it too. One of them gave me the nod and I hit the bathroom again, only this time the results were more violent. I wanted to die.

It was all too much for me and now that I was safely out of New Orleans, all of the physical and psychological assaults of the last week came crashing down. I managed to get back to my seat and settle myself enough to endure the rest of the flight.

Once we landed, I exited the plane as fast as I could and made my way out to the curb, where my daughter Kara Grace and my son, Conor, were waiting for me while Kathy and Kaitlin stayed with the car. They both flew into my arms as did Kathy and Kaitlin when they found us. I wanted to pinch myself.

On the drive home we stopped once to get coffee. When we got back in the car I told them some of my story, and again broke down in tears. They all listened quietly and each reached out and put a hand on my shoulder.

The next day, Kathy and I went for a bike ride through the vineyards near our home in Healdsburg, in the Sonoma Country wine region. Being September, the vines were heavy with grapes and harvest was only a few weeks away.

Normally, when we ride I look at the vineyards and think how beautiful, what great "scenery" to ride through. Today, however, the first thought that came to mind when I saw those grapes was, "Look at all of that food."

I was back and I knew right then, I would never be the same. Against my will I had suffered through all that Katrina had brought, but now was grateful for the experience. I had become more fully human. Without knowing it I had needed to be thrown out of my comfort zone, needed to experience deprivation, because without that, we all risk creating a world filled with people who just don't give a damn.

Katrina taught me to not let fear, a lack of courage, or the deadening impact of the "everyday" stop me from giving a damn or making my life what I want it to be.

I returned from my bike ride, took a long shower, pulled a corkscrew out of the kitchen drawer, and had a nice glass of wine sitting on the front porch with Kathy.

THIRTY

TRYING TO STEP BACK INTO MY "NORMAL" LIFE

Early October, 2005

Wouldn't life be grand if we could freeze frame Kathy and me sitting on the porch finally able to enjoy that glass of wine on my return from Katrina? It's such a pleasant image, just the two of us safely ensconced on the refuge of that front porch. End of story. But, life isn't like that. It doesn't usually wrap up that neatly, and it didn't for me.

After escaping New Orleans and getting home I thought the big challenge would be to take a few weeks to recover, and then get back to my "normal" life. I thought my story was just about my time *during* Katrina, but it very slowly began to dawn on me that my story *started* during Katrina, and it was now *ongoing.* Being in New Orleans with the normal props of life stripped away changed me in very profound ways, and I was just beginning to understand what that foreshadowed.

Getting back into the flow of normal life was a challenge. Everything seemed changed. The little things now truly seemed inconsequential and didn't bother me. I felt like I had been given a great blessing, and I could see the world much more clearly. My purpose in life, what's

141

really true and valuable was right there in the center of my heart every-day. I didn't feel that old sense of being lost or desensitized that the sheer onslaught of daily life can bring on. I had been released from the need to measure my worth by how much stuff I could accumulate.

As the days slipped by I began to experience more Katrina induced changes. My tolerance for ignorance, intellectual laziness, arrogance, and most of all for people who just don't give a damn about anything but themselves was gone. My willingness to surrender my own judg-ment and intuition to so called "authority figures" was at zero. I was unwilling to settle for anything but an authentic life of daily purpose at the same time that I wasn't even sure that was possible. I was deter-mined to not allow the demands of everyday life to possess me again.

Katrina had energized me and washed away decades of self-doubt and fear of being authentic, of speaking what was true for me. I des-perately needed to build my own internal levees that would be strong enough to keep those old negative feelings from cresting and sub-merging my authentic voice again. I wasn't going to hide myself away deep down inside anymore.

However, it was only after being home a couple of months that I realized the major change that Katrina had wrought in me; I was now on a *quest*, one that had two major goals...

- I passionately wanted to tell the world the story of what happened in New Orleans during Katrina.

- I desperately wanted to keep my true voice alive, that state of being authentic in the world and living on purpose that Katrina had given me.

However, when you go for a life of authenticity the picture that comes into focus isn't always pretty. To my horror I began to realize that I had become one of those people who *settled* for the life they had even if they were unhappy with it. I'd sworn to myself that I'd never, ever be one of *those* people. I began to understand how a person can go from being determined never to settle to finding themselves doing exactly that. When I saw myself at that point where the idea of settling *didn't seem so bad* it scared the hell out of me. It's like that movie, *Invasion of the Body Snatchers*, where you keep fighting off fatigue to keep yourself awake until at some point it seems so much easier, even appealing, to just go to sleep and let the pods take your soul.

So I was on the precipice of losing my soul, of irrevocably destroying any living connection with my true self. I was about to become a permanent member of the *surface skimmers class*, those who just skim along the surface of life avoiding the deep places and any meaningful connections. All you have to do is not think too deeply about yourself and the life that you've gotten yourself into. Just have that beer, and flip on the tube. After all, I didn't have time to focus on the important things like passion, purpose, and living a values based daily life. I kept telling myself that I'd focus on that stuff once my life settled down. Without realizing it I had hit upon the perfect formula for settling, for living an unconscious life. I could go on, but I'm sure you get the picture.

Katrina had awakened me enough to realize that I was letting myself be seduced by that *mermaid of giving up and settling*, and that recognition enabled me to turn my back on her.

So my quest was on and even though I had no idea how I was going to fulfill it I knew I had to try. I was going to write the story of what I had seen and experienced in New Orleans, and at the same time I was launching a quest to keep a firm grip on my Katrina-revealed authentic self.

Telling the story of New Orleans was going to be a much easier quest than living a life of purpose every single day. I mean, really, how do you do that? Is it even possible? It's one thing to discover your purpose, but just as big a challenge is how to stay connected to it, how not to get sidetracked by the sheer number of events in daily life that require your attention and pull you away from your core.

I had only been back from New Orleans for a month, and I was still deep into re-entry. Whenever I would tell my story to anyone they would say that the story was so compelling I had to write a book. I liked the idea, but I didn't really see myself as a writer, and I also didn't believe my story was big enough to make a whole book.

However, I couldn't let the idea go and was turning it over in my mind as to just how I could make it happen. I was looking for a way. I wasn't quite sure how to proceed, but figured a great first step would be to return to the scene of the crime; I had to go back to New Orleans.

THIRTY ONE

GETTING READY TO GO BACK TO NEW ORLEANS

Early November, 2005

I t was now early November, and I started taking the first steps in
planning a trip back to New Orleans. I was bonded to her, I needed
to be there, and I had to face the scene again. It was hard enough to
believe that what I had gone through was real and going back now
would help me keep a grip on it.

You know how it goes when something really traumatic happens
to you. While it's going on it feels real, immediate, and awful, but
as time goes on and you get further away from the event your mind
starts to play tricks on you. It starts telling you things like, "Oh
come on now, it wasn't that bad. Don't you think you're overreacting just a bit? Your life was never in danger. So it was hot, big deal!"
And so on.

Well, that's exactly what was going on inside my head about my
time during Katrina. I suffered when I was in Katrina, no doubt about
it, from the fear of the lawlessness, the stress of being trapped and
unable to leave, the uncertainty of how long I'd be there, the helpless-
ness, and most of all from the heat. New Orleans in the summer is

always hot and muggy, but with seventy-five percent of the city covered with water the humidity was just unbearable.

I'd gone through a *mental brain-washing* like this once before when my oldest daughter and I almost drowned while on vacation on Kauai. Kaitlin was seven years old, and she and I were out snorkeling when we got a little too far away from shore following the fish and being pushed out by a strong rip tide. When we discovered how far out we had drifted I put Kaitlin on my back and started swimming for shore, but the current was so strong it took all the energy I had to make any progress. After swimming for what seemed like an eternity and still being pretty far from shore, my arms began to feel like lead weights. I knew that if I wasn't able to touch bottom within the next couple of arm strokes we were going to drown.

I couldn't believe it even as it was happening to me. I could look over and see the big hotel on the beach, and it was no more than fifty yards away. I could see other people in the water, although they weren't close enough to help us. I didn't cry out for help as I didn't want to scare Kaitlin, but more fundamentally I was too embarrassed to do so. It would have been an admission of failure on my part, an admission that I had put us in this precarious position, and it was my fault. I know how that must sound to you, but those were the thoughts churning through my mind as we were two strokes away from drowning. It was an insane experience.

Just as I took my last stroke before surrendering I touched down and could feel the sandy bottom. I struggled to wade back up to the shoreline, which was still a ways away. When we got close to shore I put Kaitlin down and let her walk the last few yards. We literally crawled up and collapsed on the sand, both of us spitting up salt water that we had swallowed as we struggled against the current and the swells. As soon as we caught our breath and could talk Kaitlin asked, "Daddy what happened?"

Not wanting to scare her any further or let her know how close we had come I said, "Oh nothing Honey. We just got a little too far away from the shore."

Why do I confide this to you now? The reason is that my mind began to diminish the severity of that near drowning as time wore on just like it was doing now with my Katrina experience. It must be some sort of self-protective trick that the mind plays so that you can get on with the rest of your life and not be living the trauma of an event like that on a daily basis. In a funny way I had to go back to New Orleans to prove to myself that it had really happened.

It was now towards the end of November and in getting ready to go back I wanted to first talk to Jim Krasula, the CBS Radio reporter who had graciously welcomed me to ride out of New Orleans in his van. I wanted to let him know that I was starting the process of writing a book about my experiences in New Orleans during Katrina. But more importantly I wanted to know why Jim had taken me under his wing and delivered me from my entrapment in the denuded world that Katrina had made of New Orleans.

On December 7th I finally was able to get Jim on the phone. It was the first time we had spoken since the period right after the storm. I asked him why he had decided to let me ride out of town in his van, why he had waited with me in Kenner until I found a way to Baton Rouge, and why he had given me a beer and food and offered to let me stay with him in the van until I was safely out of town.

"Well, it was a good feeling knowing that I could help someone out of a bad situation. If I could help just one person I was doing some good," he said.

We talked some more and he told me a story of going back to New Orleans several days after he had helped me escape. "I had gone back to cover the aftermath of Katrina and I was sitting in my van parked on Canal Street when an elderly couple came shuffling up. The old woman approached my window begging for a piece of bread. I was getting tired of looking in people's eyes who had lost everything. The old woman was crying and said, 'I hate to beg sir, but could you possibly spare a piece of bread? Sir, I don't know if we'll even be alive tomorrow.'"

"I got out of the van and opened the back door and gave her bread and a few other things."

"You're an angel. This is a gift from God," she said.

"Then she hugged me. I told her, Lady, please get the hell out of here. After what I've seen I haven't cried yet and I don't want to start now."

Jim then said to me, "That's why I helped you. The whole experience of Katrina was so overwhelming and I was seeing suffering everywhere that I couldn't do anything about so when the chance came up to actually help someone I couldn't turn my back on that."

"Well, Jim, that lady was right. You are an angel. You're my guardian angel."

THIRTY TWO

MY FIRST TRIP BACK TO NEW ORLEANS

December, 2005

I n early December I made flight reservations for my first trip back. I was now scheduled to be in New Orleans from December 28th through the 31st. I booked a room at the Renaissance Pere Marquette Hotel, which is just a block over from the French Quarter. I couldn't bear to go back and stay at the Hotel Monteleone just yet.

Actually, the main reason for that first trip was to fly Kaitlin back to New Orleans after she had spent the Fall Semester at the University of San Francisco, another Jesuit university. The Loyola campus and surrounding area in New Orleans didn't suffer much damage, but with practically the entire city out of commission the decision was made to close the campus for the Fall Semester and reopen for the Winter Semester. All the students were encouraged to find other schools to attend for that Fall Semester and many other colleges gladly obliged and worked out special arrangements for Loyola students.

Kaitlin and I were both anxious to get back and see how her apartment had fared during and after the storm. We had no idea what we'd find. When Kaitlin and a couple of friends were getting ready to evacuate prior to Katrina they ran into another friend who was driving home to Houston. She invited them all to stay with her, and they gladly accepted. In Houston they watched the unfolding story of Katrina on television.

It was now just past Christmas and time to go. Kaitlin and I flew into Houston to pick up her car, Little Red. The drive from Houston to New Orleans takes about five hours, and the time passed quickly as we drove on into the night.

Driving into New Orleans I found myself feeling quite anxious and apprehensive. The biggest challenge of my life in recent times had been how to get OUT of New Orleans, and here I was willingly going back. I had no choice. Remember what I told you about the feeling of just wanting to be at home that was lodged in the middle of my heart while I was stuck during Katrina? Well, now I had a feeling of needing to be in New Orleans, needing to see it, needing to talk with others who'd been through Katrina. That feeling was now sitting on my heart and the only way that I could ease it was to be there and tell her story. I had been desperate to get out, and now I was desperate to get back in.

When we arrived it was early evening and dark already, which meant that I couldn't really see much as far as damage from Katrina. We drove out to the Garden District and made a beeline to Kaitlin's apartment to see how it had fared and if she had a habitable place to live. We arrived at the apartment and saw that a very large tree had been blown down in the front yard, but there was no other obvious damage outside. Miracle of miracles, when we entered the apartment and took a quick tour not one of those old rickety windows had blown out. I felt a sense of pride that my efforts to secure the windows before we left had contributed to keeping the apartment from suffering any major damage. So aside from the tree in the front yard and some water spots on the ceiling where the roof had leaked the apartment was fine.

Well, that's not actually quite true. There was the matter of the refrigerator. The apartment had sat empty for nearly four months, and God only knows how long it was before electricity was restored. Suffice it to say that whatever had been left in the refrigerator by now was a rotting, stinking mess. This was a major problem for just about every home in the greater New Orleans area. Everywhere we drove we saw refrigerators with their doors duct taped shut sitting out on the curb waiting for someone from the City to pick them up. Seriously, where do you dump thousands and thousands of smelly, foul refrigerators?

After assuring ourselves that everything at the apartment was okay we drove down St. Charles Avenue and stopped for dinner at VooDoo Barbecue, one of our favorite places to eat. Following that we drove down to the Pere Marquette where we turned the car over to the parking attendant and walked inside.

As we walked into the hotel we could quickly see that things weren't quite put back together yet. Where normally there would have been nice chairs and tables we saw only one card table and a couple of folding chairs with a small television set on top of the table. A security guard was sitting there watching television and paid no mind to us as we walked by. The windows were all steamed up from the great amount of moisture that Katrina had left behind. It was an eerie feeling walking through there like the place wasn't quite ready for being open, but open they were. It was like watching a dress rehearsal for a play where you get to see the actual performance, but also the rough edges, the cracks and behind the scenes.

We reached that part of the lobby where the front desk would have normally been, but there was no desk and no sign of any activity. It was just empty. We walked over to the elevators and saw a small sign that said to go to the second floor to check in. We caught the elevator and made our way to the front desk where several friendly staff members met us. As we checked in the clerk began to tell us what was and was not working in the hotel due to Katrina. I felt a need to tell her that I was there during the storm, a need to connect with her in that way.

"Oh you were here? At the Pere Marquette?" she asked.

"No, I was staying at the Monteleone, but I didn't get out until the Thursday following the storm so I know what it was like down here."

It's funny that I needed her to know that. I don't know what it was other than I was not an outsider, someone who had just come to view the storm damage or someone making a first business trip to New Orleans. I was family.

We went to our room and got ready to turn in for the night. I was amazed to have modern conveniences like electricity, running water, and air conditioning in New Orleans! After watching television and checking my email I turned the light off and settled into a fitful night of sleep.

The next morning we got up and walked over to Cafe Beignet, which is just a couple of blocks away from the Pere Marquette. It was extremely strange being out in downtown New Orleans walking around and seeing normal life resuming. It was hard for me to believe that just four short months ago this city had been under water, desperate, lawless and cut off from the rest of the country. And I had been there! So it had to be just about impossible for anyone who wasn't there to have the slightest idea of what it was like. It was simply incomprehensible.

Everywhere I looked I could see the high water marks on the buildings. In this part of town the water had risen to about three feet deep or just enough to ruin everything it touched. Most stores were still shut down, and large dumpsters sat on each block full of the remains Katrina had left behind.

Cafe Beignet is on Rue Royal, the same street as the Monteleone, which meant that we had to walk right by it. Strong feelings of desperation and disquiet came over me as we walked past her and the exact spot where four months earlier I had stood lined up waiting for the buses that never showed. As we passed the hotel my feelings roared from desperation through to disbelief. Could it really have happened as I remembered it?

After breakfast of coffee and beignets, the local doughnut like pastry, we headed back to the Pere Marquette, got Little Red and drove out to the Garden District to get Kaitlin's apartment back together. As we drove down St. Charles Ave. we passed many stores that were still boarded up including the Rite Aid where we'd stopped the Saturday before the storm and bought whatever supplies we could find including those two bottles of red wine.

Kaitlin's room was exactly as we had left it with the new bookcase face down on the floor surrounded by piles of bags of clothes and belongings. She hadn't really had a chance to move in back in August so we had work to do to get her settled. We both tackled the room and spent the entire day moving, stacking, sweeping and cleaning, and by nightfall we could begin to see the outlines of a very comfortable little room. We broke for dinner, went back to the hotel and turned in exhausted from the full day of cleaning and moving.

The next morning we drove out to a great little coffee house, Rue de la Course, which isn't far from Kaitlin's apartment and had a quick breakfast. There was a colorful sign in gold and red glitter hanging in the cafe that read, "Rebuilding New Orleans, One Party at a Time." You gotta love New Orleans.

After breakfast we went back to finish getting Kaitlin set up for school. The big, big challenge still awaited us: the refrigerator. Neither of us had dared even peek inside, fearful of what we'd find, of what might be growing in there. We had noticed flies coming from behind and circling around the refrigerator, which we took as an ominous sign. We weren't necessarily scared of looking, just freaked out by imagining what carbon-based life forms had taken hold in our absence.

Kaitlin finally broke the logjam and decided she'd give a try at cleaning it out. Her building contained three other apartments and could best be charitably described as being in the "student ghetto" owned by a man who had likely last put any money into fixing up the place during the Nixon administration. One of Kaitlin's roommates had already phoned him to ask about getting a new fridge, to which he had said no and suggested they try to clean this one up. "It should be fine," he said.

Before opening the door Kaitlin had found a blue bandana that she wrapped around her nose and the lower part of her face to help with the expected onslaught of stink. She approached the fridge with her right hand out aiming for the handle while I crept close behind her. She grabbed the handle, gave a good tug and we were hit by a four-month old wave of stench that was so powerfully indescribable that I'm not sure that we didn't both momentarily black out. You've probably had that happen. You know, you're still standing and you look like you're with it, but your mind and soul have escaped your body for a few fleeting seconds, which they can do.

Everything was suddenly moving in slow motion, even sound itself. I'm not sure if I imagined it while blacked out, but I seem to remember lunging forward to push the door closed while the word "no" escaped my lips at about quarter-speed such that it sounded more like "nooooooooooooooooooooo!" Whether that actually happened or whether Kaitlin just instinctively slammed the door shut to contain the putrid smell and the wriggling ball of flies that were dying to escape I'm still not sure to this day. Regardless, the door was now shut, but as they say, the genie was out of the bottle. The stench hung over the two of us like a black gauze curtain blotting out everything, even light.

We could actually see the stench cloud move out of the kitchen and down the hall towards her room so we knew it was too late. The better course would have been to have duct taped that baby shut then and there and had it hauled out to the curb without ever taking so much as a peek inside. But we had already chosen a path and now had billions of stinky little atoms sticking to every square inch of real estate on our bodies. And now, we were one with the stench.

The only thing we could do was to escape out of the apartment into the open air to catch our breath. However, that didn't give us much of a break as the air was so humid, and there was no breeze whatsoever. Besides, the stench cloud came with us. We just couldn't escape it.

After trying to breathe for several minutes we knew we had no choice but to move ahead so back inside we went. Kaitlin steadied herself, pulled up a chair in front of the fridge and once again opened the door. The initial explosion had taken some of the pressure off so while the stench still assaulted all our senses at least we didn't black out this time. While she pulled out bottles of mustard, ketchup, and black lumps that might have once been vegetables, meat, or even cheese for that matter, I stood behind her and held garbage bags open to receive it all. I then took the bags of methane producing slop out to the curb. I must have made four or five trips with my arms full of those garbage bags.

Once Kaitlin had cleared everything out she tried to clean the insides and despite her best efforts, nothing, not ammonia, not even Mr. Clean could do anything to cut that smell. It was just too powerful and made us feel feeble and light-headed. Besides that, it had now infected the entire apartment.

We finally had to bow to reality herself and admit that no amount of cleaning and scrubbing would ever return that old refrigerator to anything close to its former faded glory. I'm guessing it was about a 1954 model that had served generations of Loyola students. It really didn't have any sentimental value, but it had been a good comrade, soldiering on all those years making it possible for students to have barely chilled iced tea in the summers. So we closed the door one last time and duct taped her shut. Farewell, loyal friend!

By now we had spent most of the day fiddling with the refrigerator and getting the apartment ready for human habitation. Exhausted and smelling like God-knows-what we got in Little Red and drove back down to the Pere Marquette where we took turns taking nice, long, hot showers. It was only with a lot of hot water, fancy soap and scrubbing like the dickens that the smell begrudgingly began to let go of me. The more I scrubbed the more I began to think of that smell as a living thing like a virus. You know, the refrigerator had been its host and now we were the host organism, and that stink was fighting for it's little viral life.

Satisfied that we had done all we could to kill the refrigeo-viral-funk we walked over to have dinner at the Red Fish Grill on Bourbon Street. Since this was my last night in New Orleans I knew I had to go and face the Monteleone. I had to walk in that place and see her again for myself. I had to stand in that lobby where I had once been abandoned and locked in the hotel by myself.

We finished dinner and walked the short block to the Monteleone. The doorman met us with a friendly greeting and held the door open. We walked into the lobby and the whole scene was just surreal. There was absolutely no sign of the desperate conditions that had existed there just four months ago. The biggest and most obvious change was that the air conditioning was working and the joint was lit up like a grand ballroom. I mean, I knew what it had been like during Katrina. I was there, yet it was hard even for me to believe that it had really happened the way I remembered it.

We walked around the lobby and I showed Kaitlin the places that I had described to her in my story. We then headed for the Carousel Bar where we found two seats on the carousel. We sat down and ordered drinks. During the couple of times that I'd stayed at the Monteleone prior to Katrina I had gotten to know Parker, one of the bartenders. Well, at least we recognized each other, and that night Parker was the bartender on duty. We said hello and formally introduced ourselves to one another. He remembered that I had been there during Katrina so we talked about that a bit. I told him about my experience of being abandoned and locked in the hotel, and he was flabbergasted. He had not heard that story so I doubted if anyone else at the hotel had either. I hadn't spoken with any of the hotel management since the storm so there was no way anyone could have known.

Sitting in the bar and looking around at the other patrons I began to feel a strong need to tell my story to anyone who would listen. But it was more than that. I felt a sense of resentment towards the other patrons. I had been at the hotel with so many others who had suffered, and here were these people, these newcomers, who had no idea what had gone on there. They were riding the carousel smoking their cigarettes, downing their cool drinks, talking up their neighbors and enjoying the air conditioning and lights. They didn't deserve to be there now at least without knowing what had happened and appreciating how damned lucky they were. I wanted to scream at them.

I could feel myself getting more and more emotional as Kaitlin and I sat there slowly circling Parker and the other bartender. That overwhelming feeling of desperation that had lived at the center of my heart the entire time during Katrina was slowly squeezing my chest. I could also feel the fear from my Katrina experience along with the knowledge that I had been in not just an uncomfortable situation, but a very dangerous one. The topper of them all was a sweeping feeling of relief, of amazing grace, that I had made it out, and I was now safe even as I sat at ground central of my Katrina ordeal.

It was all too much and I began to cry, and I couldn't stop myself. Tears were furiously rolling down my cheeks. Kaitlin reached over and put her hand on my shoulder and softly said, "It's okay now Daddy. It's okay."

I was both embarrassed and relieved. I had found that living, breathing connection with my Katrina ordeal that I had been seeking. Yes, it had really happened. Yes, I had actually been there. Yes, it was life threatening. Yes, I suffered. Yes, I had survived. Yes, it was real and so was I.

I now realized that the only way that I could have reconfirmed for myself what I had gone through was to be sitting there in the Carousel Bar at the Hotel Monteleone. My mind couldn't play any more tricks on me. It could no longer try to rob me of the reality of what my Katrina experience was like in its effort to strip those memories of their intense emotions and weave them into the tapestry that is the story of my life.

And it wasn't just my mind doing its normal work of emotional stripping in order to move me past the trauma. There was another mental scheme going on that involves a part of me that believes that I don't really deserve to be happy. It's a side of me that is very judgmental and prejudiced towards me. Now, I know how funny that sounds, but it's true. So in addition to the normal mental weaving of a traumatic experience into my past this other part of me was trying to chip away at my Katrina reality by whispering things to me like, "you didn't have it so bad," or "look at how the poor people of New Orleans suffered and what you went through was no big deal," or "you're just being a big baby," blah, blah, blah. Being at the Carousel Bar with Kaitlin that night put a silencer on all of those judgmental voices.

Once I pulled myself together, Kaitlin and I finished our drinks and walked back over to the Pere Marquette. It had been a long two days both physically and emotionally. I had gone through too much, had been flung into a different and stark reality—in which the thin veneer of civilization was stripped away–to now let those inner voices of judgment, fear and uncertainty rob me of my voice.

My determination to write her story and live a daily life of purpose had been reconfirmed, hardened by visiting my lovely and dear New Orleans again.

THIRTY THREE

POSTSCRIPT

Thursday, November 24, 2013

I n writing about an event that happened to me some five months after Katrina I'm reminded of one of my favorite Michael Corleone quotes from Godfather III. "Every time I try to get out they pull me back in!" That pretty much sums up my feelings about being finished with any additional major life traumas as I was coasting towards February of 2006. I was still deep in reentry mode and was beginning to face up to the fact that I needed to make additional changes to further my quest to live a life of purpose.

After I returned from that first trip back to New Orleans I began to notice that I seemed more tired than usual and didn't have the same stamina. Even climbing a flight of stairs would severely wind me. I don't mean just a little out of breath, but rather having to stop and stand at the top of the stairs to breathe before I could move on my way. This had been a slowly developing problem for some time and I had ascribed it to just being out of shape. However, now it had become so extreme that I found it difficult to stand up without nearly blacking out.

Finally, just a couple of days before Valentine's Day I could barely get out of bed and decided it was time to call my doctor. When I got Steve on the phone I told him that I thought I'd need a wheelchair to get from the car to his office at the University of California, San Francisco. "Then go to the Emergency Room and I'll meet you there," he said.

I got dressed and started the climb up two flights of stairs to the street level where Kathy had the car ready. After several stops to breathe, to avoid passing out, and to throw up I made it to the car. On the drive into San Francisco I told my wife to be sure and tell my kids that I loved them. I didn't know what was wrong, but I sensed this was serious.

When we arrived at UCSF Medical Center an attendant brought out a wheelchair and wheeled me into the ER lobby. After we quickly got the registration process out of the way I was whisked into an ER room and transferred to a gurney. The ER staff immediately started an IV and drew blood to begin the process of determining what the heck was going on.

As I lay there one of the many people that attended me was a young doctor who had a clipboard with a list of questions he needed to ask me. He appeared nervous and ill at ease and fumbled over his last question which was something about what I wanted to have happen if things didn't turn out well. It sounded like he was asking me about my last wishes just in case I died, or at least that's how I took it. Looking up at him I said, "If I don't make it I want Stevie Wonder to have my eyes," which is a line from the movie *Ferris Bueller's Day Off*. He blinked his eyes, but otherwise his nervous expression remained unchanged. I guess he wasn't used to that kind of "gurney humor" from folks wheeled into the ER as bad off as I was. I just love stuff like that. You know, the absolute and complete absurdities in life.

After about an hour of waiting on that gurney the physician on duty came back in and announced that they hadn't yet been able to determine the cause, but that they'd discovered that I'd lost two-thirds of my blood. "What the hell? How is that even possible?" I thought to myself.

I was shocked and had no idea how this had happened. At the same time I was glad to know there was a reason I was feeling so puny, and it wasn't just that I was out of shape. That would have been a pretty embarrassing diagnosis. You know, you're tired and fatigued basically because you're lazy and lack any motivation!

As the ER staff prepared to admit me to the hospital we waited maybe half an hour for a bed to open up. Finally, a bed became available in what is called the "Step Down Unit," which means that it's one step down from the Intensive Care Unit (ICU).

I got wheeled upstairs and put into a room with a gentleman who had recently suffered a stroke. A nurse started the first of what would eventually become the transfusion of eight units of blood over the next couple of weeks. Still feeling weak, confused as to what was causing the blood loss, and lucky to be alive, I felt an enormous wave of gratitude for people who give blood. Those anonymous donors were saving my life.

Once I began to stabilize and my coloring started to return my doctor ordered a series of tests to determine the source of the blood loss. They knew that I was bleeding internally, but the mystery was the cause and why it had gone undetected for so long.

Several days after the testing started my doctor, Hobart, came to my room to deliver the news we'd been anxiously awaiting. "It turns out that you have a stomach tumor that is called a 'GIST' or Gastrointestinal Stromal Tumor. It has likely been slowly bleeding into your stomach for about a year, but so slow that it wouldn't have been easy to detect. That's the bad news, but the good news is that if you have to have a stomach tumor this is the best kind to have." That bit of good news provided scant comfort as I was struggling to comprehend what he was saying.

"Are you talking about cancer?" I asked with a clear edge of desperation in my voice.

"Yes, I'm sorry, but I am. I don't believe that it has metastasized so that's more good news," he said.

"Seriously? Cancer? What does that mean? What can we do?" I asked.

"Luckily, with this type tumor we think we can surgically remove it all. We will see once we open you up, but we believe that we may have to take part of your stomach along with it just to be sure."

So that was it. In the blink of an eye I had become a cancer patient. There was good news and bad news, and none of it made any sense. I had never even been in the hospital before, and suddenly here I was with stomach cancer waiting to have major surgery.

I kept turning the word "cancer" over and over in my mind trying to fit it into the category of "me," but it just wasn't working. It would take me quite a long time to weave the cancer story line into the tapestry of my life.

The surgery was successful, and my surgeon did have to take half my stomach with the tumor. After a two and a half week stay in the hospital I was finally able to go home. Recovery from the surgery would take several months, but getting my stamina back took most of the next year.

You might be wondering why I'm telling you this now. I would be, but there's a good reason I want you to know. Had I collapsed from the loss of blood like I did *during* Katrina I'm pretty confident I would have died. I know I wouldn't have been able to physically get myself to a hospital, and even if I had been able to do so there wouldn't have been any blood available to keep me alive. The nearest hospital to me was Memorial, and it was a total wreck.

Sometimes the Universe nudges us in directions that we need to go but that we may not realize or we may resist. At other times the Universe takes a sledge hammer to open our eyes to the truth of our lives. Katrina was such a sledgehammer-wake-up-call letting me know that I needed to get back to center, open my eyes to the truth of my life, and recommit myself to living on purpose.

Just in case I hadn't understood all that the sledgehammer-call from Katrina meant, the Universe delivered cancer like a stick of dynamite to blow up any remaining resistance to facing and making a number of key decisions to change the life I had settled for. I may be hard-headed, but it's pretty hard to ignore two life alerting calls like these in a short six month span. So I answered those calls.

The Universe sends us messages in a variety of ways to cut through the static of everyday life and to essentially call us back to center, to remind us of how important it is to live an authentic life, and to inspire us to live each day on purpose. One of my favorite messages from the Universe is a quotes from the Commencement Address Steve Jobs delivered at Stanford University, June 12, 2005.

"You can't connect the dots looking forward; you can only connect them looking backwards. So you have to trust that the dots will somehow connect in your future. You have to trust in something — your gut, destiny, life, karma, whatever. This approach has never let me down, and it has made all the difference in my life."

My wish for you is that you answer your own calls, and that you do so before the Universe takes a sledgehammer to your head.

Thank you so much for taking this journey with me. I love you.

Thirty Four

Leadership Lessons Learned

T he story of Katrina is one of a massive failure of leadership on all levels including local, state and federal governments along with emergency and disaster relief agencies. I strongly believe that had effective leadership been on the ground in New Orleans immediately after the storm passed much of the suffering, confusion and death could have been prevented.

My experiences during Katrina forced me to confront, understand, and fully accept my own passive dependency on authority figures to look after and free me from New Orleans. In short, part of that leadership failure was my own. However, when the New Orleans police refused to help and left me standing alone in that hotel garage it amounted to a "wake up" call. I realized that if I was going to get safely out of New Orleans it would be by my own decisions and actions. I had to take the responsibility I'd been expecting the authority figures to take and lead myself out of harm's way. All these factors combined to set the stage for me to make a *leadership switch*, and opened the door to a breakthrough in understanding five bedrock lessons about leadership that I'd like to share with you.

1) *Access, Trust, and Act on Your Gut Intuition:* The process of becoming a leader starts by engaging your own gut level leadership intuition. It's about developing your ability to *access, trust, and act on your intuition.* It's making what I call the *leadership switch,* which means switching your focus for direction from outside of yourself and from "authority figures" to inside of yourself and your own intuition. It means using your leadership intuition as a compass by which to navigate when the external landmarks aren't clear or have been washed away, literally, as they were in Katrina. This is the fundamental starting point for developing your leadership potential.

2) *Learning to be a Leader is an Experiential Process:* In order to become the best leader that you can be, you must have direct *experience* of engaging and acting on your intuition and heart. You can't only read about how to do this. I believe that directly experiencing a personal challenge, even a crisis, helps you to make that *leadership switch* and lock onto your leadership capabilities. Going through an outdoor challenge such as *Outward Bound* is an example of a program that can help you tap your native leadership instincts.

3) *The Ability to Deal With Reality is Key:* Developing the ability to deal with reality, especially a fast-changing reality, is key to successful leadership. This involves being able to switch off what you *thought would happen* to facing what is *actually happening.* Further, it means being able to shift your "internal frame of reference" to quickly match a new, changed reality. Being stuck on "this isn't what's supposed to be happening" impairs your ability to respond successfully and make reality based decisions.

4) *Without Identifying and Taking Responsibility For Your Weaknesses You Will Not Be Able to Develop Your Full Leadership Potential:* Identifying and learning to take responsibility for and/or resolve your weaknesses is essential to developing your leadership potential. Unless you do this, your weaknesses remain as hidden obstacles, much like logs floating just under the surface of a river. Such leadership blocking weaknesses may include fear, a lack of confidence, or even arrogance, among others. The central weakness I faced in Katrina was overcoming my fear of asking for help or even admitting that I needed help. Fear of dependency and of "being a burden" followed closely behind.

5) *Never Hand Over Complete Responsibility for Your Situation to "Authority Figures."* Don't naively trust authority figures as if you are trusting a Higher Power. They will do their best, but they will always have their own self-interest in mind as well, which may not align with what's best for you. Never ignore your "leadership instinct," and always hold on to some quotient of responsibility for yourself and your situation.

ABOUT THE AUTHOR

Dr. Gregory A. Ketchum

Dubbed the "Frasier of the Cubicles" by the *San Francisco Chronicle*, Dr. Greg is a former clinical psychologist-turned CEO, media expert, and executive coach. He is the CEO of *TalentPlanet®*, a leadership development firm. Dr. Greg was formerly the "CBS 5 Workplace & Career Expert" for KPIX TV Eyewitness News (CBS San Francisco) and previously hosted a weekly 2-hour call-in talk show on CNET and XM satellite radio focused on careers and the challenges of the 21st Century workplace. He is co-author of *Killer Photos With Your iPhone* (Course Technology, 2011). He lives in Muir Beach, CA. with his fiancée, Debbie.

Made in the USA
Charleston, SC
14 January 2015